THIS FREEDOM OF OURS

THIS FREEDOM
OF OURS

BY

FRANK BIRCH

CAMBRIDGE
AT THE UNIVERSITY PRESS

1937

CAMBRIDGE
UNIVERSITY PRESS

University Printing House, Cambridge CB2 8BS, United Kingdom

Published in the United States of America by Cambridge University Press, New York

Cambridge University Press is part of the University of Cambridge.

It furthers the University's mission by disseminating knowledge in the pursuit of
education, learning and research at the highest international levels of excellence.

www.cambridge.org
Information on this title: www.cambridge.org/9781107655447

© Cambridge University Press 1937

First published 1937
First paperback edition 2014

A catalogue record for this publication is available from the British Library

ISBN 978-1-107-65544-7 Paperback

CONTENTS

PREFACE

When I first undertook this series of "talks" I was staggered by the size of the subject and the multitude of its ramifications and I cast about for some authority to guide me in my planning. Dicey, for instance— surely someone must have "brought him up to date". I consulted libraries, bookshops, friends. But to no purpose. There was literature enough and to spare covering each of the several fields over which my subject ranged, but apparently none had recently covered the whole ground.

And to cover the whole ground I was determined. That was essential. Freedom was on its trial. There was plenty of advocacy current on either side, but very little attention was being paid to the evidence. Everyone talked about freedom, but hardly anyone seemed to know what he was talking about.

What then exactly was this freedom of ours? It was unique—not necessarily better or worse than any other variety, but different. It had grown up with the nation. Its peculiarity, therefore, could only be made clear in the light of the nation's history— religious, political, social and economic. History would explain its nature. Then law would define its extent. But not entirely. For the law is one thing on paper, another in practice; and the difference would only be revealed by enquiry into the administration of justice. Lastly, such as it was, was it worth while? Could it be bettered? Did the necessary machinery exist, and were conditions favourable, for its betterment? Or was freedom an illusion—unattainable, or, perhaps, not even worth attaining? If so, what were the alternatives?

That was the ground I set myself to cover in ten periods of half an hour plus one of twenty minutes. And the task was not made easier by the fact that when I started to examine the evidence, I did not know to what conclusions that evidence would drive me. Had I known, I should have consciously planned the argument to lead up to—and, probably, to bolster up—these conclusions. So, in confessing two faults, I plead two excuses. If I have tried to cram too much into too small a space, it is because the job was not worth doing at all unless it was done completely; and if the treatment is badly planned, it is because I approached the subject with—as far as is humanly possible—an open mind.

If you (not being a cook) have ever tried to make a complicated and unfamiliar dish with no other guidance than that of the cookery book, you will know what I felt about these "talks". I knew all the ingredients; I mixed them faithfully in the proper proportions; but I didn't know exactly what sort of pudding would result. It turned out rather unexpectedly. The *taste* was all right—to *me*—perhaps because I had made it myself. But it *looked* a bit odd —clumsy, misshapen. And I'm not sure how far it is fit for general consumption. To some it may be indigestible; to others unpalatable. All I can say is that it came out like that. And though I may not have succeeded in presenting freedom very well, I have at least discussed and analysed the ingredients of which it is composed. And that in the main is all I set out to do.

For me the work was an experiment—a genuine voyage of discovery. And in the end I discovered the obvious. Unexpected it was, as I say, but obvious. At least, so it seems to me now. But it didn't before. And to judge by what one reads and hears daily, it still isn't obvious to many. It can't be anyway to the old-fashioned Individualist, nor to the doctrinaire Socialist, and it admittedly isn't to the Communist or Fascist. And inasmuch as "talks" delivered at weekly intervals, each of them self-contained, afford no opportunity for a summary of findings, let me take this last chance of summarising the Obvious which I discovered.

Those who disapprove of Despotism as a form of government condemn it as being evil *in itself*, as well as for its results. But I notice that the worst modern enemies of Democracy do not attack its nature but its functioning. It is, they say, inefficient. It won't work. By which they mean really that it didn't, wouldn't, or couldn't be made to work in their own countries. About that they may be right, or they may be wrong. The point is that, even if they are right, the reason why it won't work is that they don't know how to work it.

Democracy is admittedly the hardest form of government to work. It asks, as I remark elsewhere, so much of so many. Ideally, it postulates responsibility, sound judgment, tolerance, honesty, even disinterestedness in every citizen. These can only be achieved bit by bit, gradually, by training and practice. It takes time. That is why the democracies of gradual growth and longest standing are the most successful. But in the nineteenth century, in the first flush of triumph of "liberal" ideas, democracy was optimistically regarded—and universally recommended—as a sort of ready-made garment that any nation could procure and put on at a moment's notice. And some who did put it on found it a misfit.

Then came the War—the war "to make the world

safe for democracy". Social conditions had been bad enough before. The war, the peace and the aftermath combined to make them in some countries intolerable. The disillusionment was bitter and widespread. The older democracies began belatedly to put their houses in order, but some of the younger democracies, which lacked training, experience and historical background, collapsed under the strain. Nations that couldn't work their democracies had to fall back on something else that *would* work. And Russia that had *never* known democracy swapped one form of tyranny for another. Some turned to the right, some to the left. But all alike had to adopt the only form of government that needs *no* training and which can, therefore, be assumed at a moment's notice—the most primitive form of all—Despotism.

The word democracy means government by the people. But it hasn't always been used in that sense. To the ancient Greeks, who invented the word, it meant government by a minority of citizens over a majority of non-citizens and slaves. To nineteenth-century Europe it meant government by the middle classes. It is only in the twentieth that it is coming to mean government by the manhood of the nation or, as in this country, government by all adults.

Similarly, the words freedom and liberty have changed their meaning. In this country, at any rate, liberty in mediaeval times meant the privileges of a few; later it came to mean the rights of many; now it is *supposed* to be the equal possession of all. The terms have also become more comprehensive. They have expanded to include civil, religious, political and social freedom in successive stages. We in this country have more or less completed the third stage. Civil, religious and political freedom (with reservations) are ours. We are only beginning to achieve social freedom.

And, just as democracy requires training and practice, so also does freedom. It, too, postulates responsibility, etc., in those who possess it. But it, too, was regarded in the nineteenth century as a ready-made article that could, and should, be handed out all round. Those who got it suddenly weren't used to it; weren't, therefore, capable of using it; they abused it. It has always been so. The sudden emancipation of masses of slaves resulted temporarily in chaos; the granting of even a modicum of religious liberty, before people were used to it, produced licence and abuse; political liberty, granted suddenly to inexperienced nations, led to inefficiency and corruption. Freedom is heady stuff. You've got to get used to it gradually. Some countries can stand a lot of it, some less, and some have recently lost all they ever had. We in England pride ourselves on our use of it. But with the Public Order Act (1936) we have had to surrender a bit of it, because a few of us abused that bit.

The meaning of liberty and the amount of it varied according to the requirements of those who for the time being possessed political power. Marx would substitute "economic" for "political". But that is just another of his half-truths. Economic power *tends* to identify itself with political power, but seldom, if ever, in history have they been completely identical. The simple truth is that those who possess political power control the law-making machine (in this country Parliament), and it is the law-making machine that makes freedom. The whole of our past history illustrates this truth, and recent events confirm it. In the nineteenth century political power passed gradually—the Reform Acts were the milestones—to the people. The process was carried a stage farther in 1918 and completed in 1928. The expansion of the meaning and extent of freedom closely reflected the expansion of the franchise. But only since 1928 have we been a true democracy, for only since 1928 have we had government by the whole people. And it is only since then that the people as a whole have been in a position to make freedom mean and be what the people as a whole require it to mean and be.

So when Fascists declare that democracies are decadent and that freedom is folly, or when Communists profess that both are a mockery without preliminary revolution, bloodshed, persecution and an unlimited period of dictatorship, I am not greatly impressed. Give democracy a chance. Our own is less than ten years old. There are many things to be ashamed of in this country. But, demonstrably, there are at least as many in Fascist and Communist countries. And if we look back even to the beginning of this century, when our democracy was still in the making, we can't help being impressed at the progress that has been made in spite of war and depressions and rumours of war. Indeed, there seems to me every ground for optimism. Not one of the trained democracies has collapsed; only some of the bogus and inexperienced. The survivors outnumber the casualties. They make a fine list of nations. We're in good company.

Whether freedom is good for all peoples it is not for me to say. For some it may be bad temporarily because they lack the necessary training, for others permanently because it is contrary to their upbringing and traditions. That's not *my* business—nor *any* foreigner's. But if some nations cannot stand it because they don't know how to use it, and if others have no use for it anyhow, those nations who have known how to use it will not, I think, lightly forgo its use or stand for its surrender.

And now here they all are—these "talks"—
published (with only the slightest of alterations) as
a book. But they were meant, please remember, to
be listened to in instalments, not read straight on
end. Even that doesn't account completely for their
form. A lecture, or a speech, is normally addressed
to people interested in, and familiar with, the subject.
A telephone call is addressed to someone who knows
the speaker, or, at least, his business. But the B.B.C.
talker may have got a wrong number. He can take
nothing for granted with his audience.

Many people have helped me, and I am grateful
to them all; especially to Miss Crowther-Smith of
the National Council for Civil Liberties for her
patience and kindness in answering questions, digging
out material and verifying references; to Mr John
Saltmarsh of King's College, Cambridge, for valuable
advice on various historical matters; to Mr J. B.
Herbert of the Inner Temple for vetting certain
statements about points of law; to Messrs W. Heffer
& Sons, Cambridge, for their great labour and in-
genuity in tracking down books; and above all to
Mr N. G. Luker of the B.B.C. He fathered without
bullying me, and mothered me without fussing. As
in a nursery, he taught me to "talk"; as in a school-
room, he taught me composition; and no man could
hope or wish for a better tutor, counsellor and (if I

may say so) friend. Many may have thought the series bad, but only he and I know how much worse it would have been without his guidance and collaboration.

FRANK BIRCH

London
27 *February* 1937

I

OUR TRADITION OF FREEDOM

Wʜᴀᴛ do we *mean* by "Freedom"? What do *you* mean by "being free"? I always resent being asked that sort of question myself and dislike the man who asks it. We all know him: the sort that catches you by a coat-button, if you are standing, or taps you on the knee with his forefinger, if you are sitting. It makes you uncomfortable; it compels you to think straight about something which is all confused and tangled in your mind. It was asking tiresome questions like this that made Socrates so intolerable that the Athenians put him to death.

And, of course, the true meaning of freedom is a very abstruse problem. It is also highly controversial. But the fact that we can't easily define liberty is no reason why we shouldn't discuss it or use it. Good heavens, if the human race might only use and discuss the things it could define, where should we all be? We can't define electricity, but we all use it, and by using it and discussing it we improve both its uses and our understanding of it.

That is why I have no patience with the cynics who coin phrases, such as: "The only freedom we possess is to breathe gently through the nose"—nor with the lazy-minded who cloak their laziness with cheap pessimism: "Look at our freedom!" they say. "It's all talk. One man loses his job because he *joins* a trade union: another may lose his job because he *won't* join a trade union." True. But only the fool says in his heart: "There is no freedom."

There is. Oh! granted that our liberty is incomplete, partly bogus, frequently nullified by poverty and unemployment. The more we realise its failures, the more determined we should be to make it a success. It cannot be denied in the face of history that we have more freedom than we had, nor that what we have is of better quality. We shall never attain to perfect freedom, any more than we shall ever attain to perfect goodness, because, apart from our human frailty, as fast as we progress we get a better *conception* of goodness, a higher *ideal* of freedom. Practice never makes perfect, but better practice makes us conceive a better perfection. So the freedom we have never catches up with our ideal of it. But the more honest thought we give to it, the better it will be. And, contrariwise, if we ignore it and let it go by default, as sure as eggs is eggs it will decay and dwindle and disappear. For, as Lord Macmillan reminded us recently: The price of liberty is eternal vigilance.

I am not out for a *definition* of freedom. All I want is something to *go* on, so that we may all use the word in the same sense. What does the ordinary citizen of this country mean when he talks of being free, the ordinary, average citizen—the proverbial, but elusive, "man in the street"? Well, of course, it requires a good deal of courage to stop a man in the street and ask him a question like this. He almost certainly won't like it, and his answer will probably not be to the point.

However, not long ago chance gave me the opportunity at a bus-stop in the Strand. It was during the rush-hour, and there was a crowd waiting to catch buses home. A street hawker was making the most of the occasion by demonstrating on the pavement the performance of his clock-work mice. He certainly added to the confusion. A policeman, quite good-humouredly, asked him to move on. The hawker did so, but, as he did so, shouted over his shoulder:

"This is a free country, ain't it?"

The end of his remark brought him alongside me. I seized my opportunity.

"What do you mean by 'being free'?" I asked.

He scowled at me suspiciously.

"What d'ye mean by being free?"

"I asked *you*," I said.

"Not being messed about," he answered. "That's what I mean. Not being messed about."

"Who by?" I ventured.

"Government," he said. And then, after a pause, catching sight of the policeman's back, "—and *coppers*".

I had got my answer, and I think it was the right one. "Not being messed about—by Government or coppers." I think that is really about all that is in the mind of most of us when we talk of being free. In other words, *we take our freedom for granted, except when it is interfered with.*

Unless it is interfered with, we don't give it a thought. That hawker resented being moved on for obstructing the pavement just at the one hour of the day when he stood the best chance of selling his wares. *I*, similarly, am kept at my place of work till eleven o'clock at night. Some nights I am very tired, and I should dearly like to have a drink before I go home to bed. I know for a fact that it would do me good. But I can't have it unless I have a sandwich as well—a sandwich I don't want, which I have to pay for and which, if I do eat it in order to get my money's worth, will, I know from experience, give me tummy-ache for the rest of the night. *You*, perhaps, live in the provinces. Sunday evening may be your only

4

free evening. You would like a little relaxation, a little quiet entertainment—the pictures, in fact. Nothing in your religious convictions prevents you going. But you *can't* go. The cinemas are shut. Yet in London and some other towns you *could* go. Is that fair? You and I ask the same question as the hawker asked the policeman: "Is this a free country?" But to all the things we *can* do, to all the freedom we possess and exercise daily and all day—to all this we don't give a thought. Why? Because we take it for granted.

And *why*, you may well ask, why the dickens *should* we think about it? Why shouldn't we take it for granted until it is challenged?—Ah, but it is being challenged. I'm not referring to any aspect of government policy or to the activities of any particular groups in this country. I am thinking of the challenge from abroad. There, new political philosophies are being preached that laugh at our conceptions of freedom as something ludicrously obsolete; and new forms of government have appeared under which anything like our sort of freedom simply doesn't exist. You can't open your newspaper without reading of Fascism, of Communism, of the triumph of Dictatorship and of the downfall of Democracy. Some of us dislike these innovations. Most of us hate the excesses that accompanied their birth and the arbitrary acts by which they maintain their existence. But we can't just say:

5

"Disgusting!" and shut our eyes. The most prejudiced amongst us must surely admit by now that several of these governments have achieved stability and permanence, and that each of them has done *some* good to its country. We are not paying much of a compliment to our own methods if we refuse to accept the challenge. Surely it is up to us to examine our own methods, so that we can compare them with these others and come to an honest conclusion as to which is best *for us* and why.

Please note that I say "best *for us*". Nothing is so mischief-making as the complacency with which some people and nations assume that what is good for them must be good for, and should be imposed upon, everyone else. We all know of people with certain religious scruples, or with convictions about food and drink, who would if they could—and sometimes they can—compel others, who do not share their scruples and convictions, to conform to their particular line of conduct. And, of course, in foreign relationships this self-righteousness is far more dangerous. For obviously one nation's meat may be another nation's poison.

The collapse of so many liberal democracies in modern times is a case in point. In the last century, as one nation after another shook off the yoke of despotic rule, it looked round for free institutions to set up in its place. The two shining examples were

6

the constitutions of Great Britain and the United States—the two branches of the Anglo-Saxon tradition. It copied one, or the other, or both and expected to achieve the same results. But the *tradition* could not be transplanted, and the brand-new constitutions had no roots in the countries of their adoption. You can't make a lawn in a day by just planting grass. You must water and weed and cut and roll it for years, perhaps for generations. That was the trouble. The Anglo-Saxon superstructures sat uneasily on top of alien foundations. They looked well. But they didn't fit. They wouldn't work. They weren't, as I say, *in the tradition*. They were alien, and they remained alien, and so they collapsed. And, as the Duchess said to Alice in Wonderland, the moral of *that* is, that in examining our own notions of freedom and comparing them with those of other nations, we must not jump to the conclusion that what is undoubtedly good for them would be necessarily good for us, nor smugly assume that what is good for us would be necessarily good for them.

And we, living in a democracy, are under a particular obligation to think clearly about these matters. For in a democracy the will of every citizen is consulted. Under a dictatorship no one is consulted —except the few individuals the dictator likes to consult. The citizen can still presumably *think* as he likes, but it doesn't matter what he thinks, because his speech and actions in public must conform to the will of the dictator. *He has surrendered his responsibility.* We in our democracy have not. Every one of us is consulted; therefore every one of us is responsible; and the success of our democracy depends finally on the way we face up to that responsibility—in other words, on the soundness of the judgment of each and all of us.

And it isn't always easy to form a sound judgment. Most of the problems of the day are so complicated and technical. They are matters for experts. Most of us at the best can only hope to be intelligent amateurs. We review the evidence and take the best advice. But evidence can be juggled with, and the advice offered isn't always the best. This is the great danger of democracy, that it is exposed at its weakest spot to every form of clap-trap and one-sided propaganda. We all know about the demagogue and the tub-thumping charlatan. We have all heard vaguely about undue influence from rich and powerful combines and groups. But even the best guarantees of democracy—representative institutions, for instance, and a free press—even these may imperil the integrity of our judgment. The candidate for Parliament may appeal to our baser motives; at election time at any rate he will tell us what is palatable rather than the

8

whole, naked truth. Our favourite newspaper—we like it, perhaps, for quite other reasons than its political views—by emphasising some news, suppressing or back-paging other news and interpreting the whole with a particular bias, may completely warp our judgment.

What we are told many times, and what we see often in print, whether it be true or not, we soon believe to be true. The art of propaganda is here on all fours with the art of advertisement. If we see on the hoardings every day of our life a beautiful lady holding a bar of soap, the beauty of the lady not only helps us to remember the name of that soap, but in time in our minds her beauty becomes confused with the quality of that soap; we never consciously *think* that the soap must be good because the lady is beautiful, but we are led to act as if it were so.

After all, we are busy with our own private affairs. We haven't much time to give to public affairs. And a slogan, a catch-phrase, a half-truth, save so much trouble. That is why democracy is the hardest form of government to work. It asks so much of so many: tolerance, disinterestedness, honesty of mind, sound judgment. But it is hardly too much to say that anyone in this country to-day who shirks the challenge to free institutions abroad, who can't be bothered to examine our own brand of freedom, or who approaches the subject with a hopelessly biased mind—every such person offers in himself an instance and a piece of evidence that democracy is bad.

But in taking stock of our freedom, how are we to proceed? Are we going to inquire just how much of it there is—measure it off, as it were, with a tape and find at the end that there is too much or too little? I hope not. It would be a long and tedious job. Take only one instance—Freedom in Business. To measure that alone we should have to plough through the whole of company law. Nor would it help much. For obviously freedom is not to be justified merely by its quantity. If we were allowed to cut each other's throats, that would add to the quantity of our freedom, but certainly not to its quality. And surely it's the *quality* rather than the *quantity* that we want to discover. Of what *value* is it? What are the principles, if any, on which it is based and limited? Is it reactionary, or stagnant, or progressive? Is it a standardised article, like a hat, which any nation, as it were, could buy in a shop, and which at some time or other we have stuck on our heads and could any day as easily discard for any other cap of liberty? Or is it something peculiar to ourselves, a part of our national personality, so intimately bound up with our past and present growth that to eradicate it would be a difficult and dangerous operation? And even if it is so, is it in a healthy condition, or should we submit it to the surgeon's knife? In short, *what is it worth—to us?* Is it just a piece of old-fashioned machinery that we obstinately cling to in the face of far better modern inventions, or is it, perhaps, ancient in origin, but up-to-date in its development and capable of still further progressive improvement in the future? Are we, in fact, a hopelessly conservative nation entangled in an outworn tradition, or is it just possible—between you and me and the microphone—is it just possible that we've got that little something the others haven't got?

When you come to think of it, it is odd anyhow that we should take our freedom for granted. It is not guaranteed by any constitutional document. To the citizens of most democracies liberty is guaranteed by an article of the constitution, and the constitutional law is regarded as sacrosanct and alterable only by special machinery difficult to set in motion. In the U.S.A., for instance, an amendment to the constitution requires the approval of two-thirds of the members of each house of Congress, followed by the agreement of three-fourths of the States. But in Great Britain we have no such rigid constitution. Indeed, we have no *written* constitution at all. All our laws are on the same footing, whether they concern dog-licences or the succession to the throne. The King in Parliament is the absolute legal sovereign and can, as has been said, do anything except make a man a woman or bind a *future* Parliament.

An Act of Parliament could abolish all our liberties in a single day. There is actually little danger of such a thing happening because, through the extension of the franchise, we have come to control the House of Commons, which itself, in the course of time, has become the preponderant partner in Parliament. But we have no constitutional guarantee for our freedom, because we have no defined constitution.

The student of the British constitution has to dig out the relevant statutes from the general body of the law. And even then his work has barely begun. About the Prime Minister, for instance, the only thing the Statute Book will tell him is that someone with that title has a certain precedence in processions, and about the Cabinet he won't find anything at all. Why? Because our constitution works according to custom as much as, if not more than, according to law.

Of course, behind every constitutional custom there is eventually a legal sanction that can at the last resort be brought into play. For instance, if the Prime Minister and Cabinet refused to resign after repeated defeats in the House of Commons, the House could eventually enforce resignation by refusing to vote supplies and thus making it impossible for the government to carry on through lack of funds. But the fact remains that it is *custom*, not *law*, that makes a ministry resign when it has lost the confidence of the House. It is true, too, that a bad breach of custom is often followed by the passage of a statute which turns that custom into law and defines—and perhaps restricts—the powers of the offender. Thus the Parliament Act of 1911 restricted the powers of the House of Lords in consequence of their rejection of the Budget of 1909. But though the volume of statutes relating to the constitution grows larger with time, the custom of the constitution is also continuously growing. There is no prospect of the one overtaking the other. And we shall never understand anything either about our constitution, or about the nature and quality of our freedom, unless we realise the importance that custom, as distinct from law, has played and still plays in our national life.

We have never been very good at inventing institutions. Our whole history is strewn with failures. Take two examples—one past, one present. The Commonwealth, which at the end of the Civil War of the mid-seventeenth century, swept away King, Lords and Commons, produced a succession of carefully thought-out new constitutions. None of them worked. And each in turn tended to resemble more closely the

old constitution. The Parliament Act of 1911, re-
stricting the powers of the House of Lords, was passed
as a temporary measure pending a promised recon-
struction of that House. But the Act still remains in
force because few can agree on a better.

But, if we can't *invent* institutions, by goodness we
can make them work! We can grow them from
insignificance to greatness; when they fail of their
original purpose we know how to adapt them to
another; and when at last they can serve no more, we
make "dead forms serve living forces". Our constitution is a thousand years old. Every bit of it has
changed almost beyond recognition. But very little
of it has ever been abolished. For in this country old
institutions are like old soldiers—They never die, they
only fade away.

As with our constitution, so with our freedom. It
was no sudden invention. It was not the result of a
revolution. It is part of the ordinary law of the land
and evolved gradually and continuously with that
law from humble beginnings. For our system of law,
with very small exceptions, is of purely native growth.
In that respect it is unique, at least in Western Europe.
In its earliest form it consisted of local, tribal or
national customs. It was, in fact, Customary Law.
In course of time, as the country became united and
government more centralised, local differences were

smoothed out and Customary Law consolidated into one code for the whole country. It was the Custom of the Country. And this custom of the country was the beginnings of the Common Law. So, too, our particular brand of freedom is of purely native growth. It, too, is the Custom of the Country. For the seed of it was already germinating in that primitive Customary Law, and as the Common Law grew to maturity, so did the freedom embedded in it. It follows, therefore, that any inquiry into its nature and quality must primarily be historical. For our freedom is not the logical expression of any school of political philosophy, but part and parcel of our national growth.

Very well then. If the investigation is to be historical, how shall we tackle it? The usual method is to divide liberty into rather arbitrary compartments, such as freedom of conscience, freedom of speech, freedom of association, and so on, and to deal with each in turn. But this procedure seems to me unsatisfactory for two reasons. In the first place, these individual "freedoms" were not achieved separately one after another. They evolved to a large extent simultaneously, and therefore to deal with each separately would involve a lot of historical repetition. And in the second place, the method itself seems to me radically wrong. It puts a wrong construction on

15

the whole subject. I can explain my meaning best, perhaps, by comparing our continuous national growth with the growth of a human being.

A man's freedom is not a *physical* part of him. He is not born with it. As he grows up he achieves it by stages. At a certain age he will get the right to wear trousers; later on, the right to smoke; and later still, perhaps, the right to a latchkey. Now, if our national freedom had been something similarly separate and distinct from our national growth, something external to it, that we achieved one bit at a time, piecemeal, we should be justified in taking one bit of freedom at a time—freedom of speech, for instance—discussing it and passing on to the next bit of freedom. But we can't do so, because the growth of our freedom was not separate from, but part of, our national growth. Our freedom was there, I said, in embryo at the very beginning of things. Our baby freedom was an inherent part of our baby nation. Of course, some aspects of freedom developed sooner, or more quickly, than others, just as a baby can walk before it can talk. A baby achieves, if you like, freedom of movement before freedom of speech. It is true, too, that some aspects of freedom are not apparent at all at that infantile stage of the nation. Still, potentially they exist, and in due time they will appear, because of other things that are there already. There is no trace of

16

beard on a baby boy's chin. But it will come—in time.

Ah! you may exclaim at this point, my metaphor is pushing my argument too far. Granted that our freedom is an inherent part of our national growth, that doesn't mean that its growth was entirely unconscious.

You are right, of course. It wasn't. I think for the *most* part it *was*—as unconscious, say, as a child's learning to walk or to talk. But at times, no doubt, when someone or something obstructed the growth of our national freedom, the process became very self-conscious indeed. Still, I don't think that spoils my argument—*or* my metaphor. In fact, if you don't mind, I will go on with both.

The growth of a healthy child proceeds naturally and subconsciously, doesn't it? But even the healthiest child falls ill sometimes, and we have consciously to apply an artificial remedy—the doctor's medicine or the surgeon's knife. So in the history of our body politic, whenever the natural growth of our freedom has been obstructed, we have had recourse to artificial remedies and reforms.

But I don't think we can take as much credit for what we have *consciously* accomplished as for what we have unconsciously evolved. Take, for example, what are, I suppose, the two best-known artificially contrived props of our freedom—Magna Carta and the Habeas Corpus Act. Magna Carta, from one point of view at least, was a reactionary feudal document most foxily misinterpreted by seventeenth-century lawyers to suit their own ends; and the Habeas Corpus Act of 1679 only passed into law, we are told, because the tellers in the House of Lords were drunk and by way of a joke counted one fat lord as ten. Or take the best known of our champions of liberty— John Wilkes. Well, well! To put it mildly, you couldn't call him a *good* man.

Anyhow, I think we can now understand why people in this country take their freedom for granted, except when it is interfered with. They have always done so. And they have done so because their freedom is an inherent part of their national growth, evolving subconsciously except when it meets with obstruction.

But obstruction by what, or by whom? Well, I asked the street hawker that question. What was his answer? "By Government," he said—"and coppers." And I don't think he meant merely the Cabinet and Policemen. He was speaking generally. He meant surely *authority and its minions*. Any authority—Church, King, Parliament and Courts of Law—the chief organs, in fact—the head, heart, lungs, and so forth, of the body politic. As long as they all functioned and grew normally and harmoniously together, the freedom that

18

was part of them grew also, healthily and subconsciously. But when any of them became defective, or failed to adapt itself to the growth of the rest, freedom suffered with the rest of the body, and a more or less drastic remedy had to be discovered and applied. So, instead of splitting up our freedom arbitrarily into fragments and examining each fragment in turn, I propose to keep it whole and see how it developed in relation to each of these authorities.

I shall attempt to show how Church, Government, Parliament, and so on, assumed their modern shape and to trace, at the same time, the ideas and principles that modelled our freedom into its present form. That will give us the *nature* of our freedom. We shall know what it is and why it is what it is. We can then discuss its *quality* and ask ourselves the final question whether what it is is worth while.

My programme then is historical to start with and only gradually becomes less so. I make no apology for that. I want to give you not my own views on liberty, so much as a sound basis on which you can discuss it for yourselves. The subject has become rather a byword for vague generalisations and high-flown platitudes. But our particular brand of freedom is only intelligible against the background of its history, and it is neglect of that history, I think, that has led to so much misunderstanding of it and to so

19   2-2

much nonsense being talked about it to-day. It may help some people to wave a red flag and shout about "the Rights of Man". It may help others to wave a Union Jack and sing how "Britons never shall be slaves". But Freedom in this country was not, thank goodness, based on anything so nebulous as "the rights of man". It had nothing to do with "ruling the waves" or "a far-flung empire". It is not with us an abstract right, but something very concrete, embedded in our laws and customs. Freedom—this Freedom of Ours—began very humbly, grew very slowly, and was fostered—and sometimes fought for— with a great deal of patience and endurance and courage, by generation after generation of our ancestors. Surely it is worth a little effort on our part to understand, to preserve and to improve.

II

FREEDOM AND THE CHURCH

" *The English Church shall be free.*" That is the
first clause of Magna Carta. It sounds good, doesn't
it? Our religious liberty guaranteed over seven
hundred years ago! What a country! What a
nation!

Unfortunately the clause won't bear that construction. Freedom didn't mean then what it means now.
It meant the special rights of a few, not the general
rights of all. It was not an ideal, as it is now, but
something very material, like a piece of property.
Certain persons, or classes of persons, and certain
places possessed certain "liberties". The baron had
his liberties by virtue of his tenure; a town had its
liberties by virtue of its charter. And these liberties,
whatever they might be, implied so much exemption
from royal or national interference—the right to
jurisdiction over your tenants, for instance; or the
right to hold a market and levy toll on its frequenters.
In short, liberty did not mean freedom, but *a* liberty
meant *a* privilege.

That was why such a fuss was made about them in Magna Carta. For Magna Carta was imposed on King John by those who possessed privileges and thought they were in danger of losing them. And that is why Magna Carta has been aptly described as the Great Charter of liberties, but not of liberty. And when, a century later, the Commons began to have a say in such matters, they begged the King in 1348 to grant no more liberties in future. For the grant of every liberty meant the removal of something from the rule of Common Law and its transfer to somebody's private jurisdiction.[1]

But our freedom is based on Common Law. Therefore, our freedom depended on the victory of Common Law over these privileges. And if we want to see how these ancient "liberties" were transformed into our modern liberty, we can't do better than start with the Church. For the Church possessed the greatest immunities and privileges of all, and what it was after in Magna Carta—and *got*—was a formal recognition of them.

The Church derived its liberties from its peculiar relationship to the State. After the Roman Empire had adopted Christianity, the Bishop of Rome, as Pope, became Head of the Church, just as the Emperor was Head of the State. The Empire later

[1] Cf. Pollard, *The Evolution of Parliament*, pp. 166–171.

broke up into fragments, but the Church didn't. So the old theory merely adapted itself to the new facts. Temporal affairs in *each* country were the business of the ruler of that country, but spiritual affairs in *every* country were the business of the Pope. Thus, there was no Church *of* England; there was only the Church *in* England—a portion of the Church Universal—or rather, strictly speaking, *two* portions, for the Church in England was divided into two provinces, Canterbury and York.

The laity had its officers of State, its Common Law, its Courts, its Councils and its Parliament, at the head of which was the King. The clergy had its hierarchy, its Canon Law and its Convocations, at the head of which was the Pope.

In theory, the division was simple. In practice, it led to endless wrangling between King and Pope, till by a fairly steady compromise the Church in England secured a measure of Home Rule.

But as England grew to nationhood, papal power came to look like foreign interference. Was not the King to be master in his own country? And what about papal taxation of the clergy—Annates and First-Fruits and Tenths—to say nothing of papal exactions from the laity, such as Peter's Pence? Good English money sent as tribute to a foreign potentate! Was England a free country? The old question.

Yes, said Parliament in 1399, in all times past so free that neither Pope nor any other outside the realm had a right to meddle therewith.

Moreover, the Church was luxurious, worldly and lazy. The nobility was jealous of it, and the poor, hard hit by the endless French Wars, felt equally bitter. Discontent found a leader in John Wyclif, Master of Balliol College, Oxford. He attacked the corruption of the Church; he translated the Bible; he even dared to deny the doctrine of transubstantiation. But that was heresy. The Church demanded its suppression. That was difficult. In the ecclesiastical courts heresy was punishable only with excommunication, and the Common Law, to its credit, made no provision for it at all. But the Lancastrian Kings needed the Church's support, so in 1401 and 1414 statutes were passed whereby heretics were to be burnt. It was under these statutes that most of the martyrs suffered during the next century and a half, and more especially under Mary Tudor.

They were repealed on Elizabeth's accession, and we ought to distinguish between these heresy laws to protect doctrine and the later penal laws against Roman Catholics and Protestants to protect the State.

But though in the fourteenth century Lollardy was driven underground, it was not crushed out. On the surface for the time being attacks on the Church were limited to its temporalities, that is, to its worldly possessions, but more radical opposition was only biding its time.

When at last that time came, however, the movement started from above, not from below—and from the most unexpected quarter. Henry VIII was a champion of orthodoxy. He had published a book refuting the doctrines of Luther and had been rewarded by the Pope with the title of Defender of the Faith. He was the last person you would expect to attack the papal power. But Henry wanted to get rid of his wife, Katherine of Aragon. He wanted Anne Boleyn; and he wanted a male heir. None of these things had anything to do with religion, yet they were the *immediate* cause of the Reformation in England. For Henry had a conscience—the sort of conscience that only a supreme egotist could have. "God and my conscience", he once said, "are on very good terms." And his conscience was now troubled, he said, because eighteen years ago he had married Katherine, who had previously been his deceased brother's wife, a union forbidden in the Book of Leviticus. Of course, he had had a dispensation from the Pope to do so. But was that dispensation valid? And anyway, couldn't he have another one now to declare the marriage void and enable him to marry again? Unfortunately for him Rome had just been sacked by the troops of the Emperor Charles V. The Pope was, therefore, at the Emperor's mercy. And Charles was a nephew of the English Queen. He naturally wouldn't stand for any insults to Aunt Katherine.

The only thing for Henry to do was to frighten the Pope into submission. So one by one in the years that followed the rights of the Pope in England were destroyed by successive Acts of Parliament. And, as the Pope remained obstinate, Henry did not stop till papal authority in this country had been completely abolished and transferred to the Crown. The clergy made their submission and Parliament formally acknowledged Henry as "Supreme Head of the Church of England".

To get his divorce he had nationalised the Church. But he made little or no doctrinal changes. He was no Lollard. Not he. He racked and burnt even women for denying the doctrine of transubstantiation. He remained orthodox to the day of his death.

But, willy-nilly, he had started the Reformation movement in England. Most people probably at that moment were content to be Catholics without the Pope. But the doctrines of the foreign reformers, Luther and Calvin, were spreading. In the two short reigns that followed, the pendulum swung violently to extreme Protestantism and back again. The regency Councils of the boy King, Edward VI, plumped for

Protestantism and plundered the Church. Mary restored Catholicism and the papal power, burnt three hundred martyrs in three years and married that arch-champion of Catholicism, Philip II, who used England as a pawn of Spain.

So, when Elizabeth succeeded to the throne, Protestant rule stood for robbery and greed, Roman Catholic rule for cruelty and national humiliation. What settlement, then, would command the widest assent? Obviously a compromise between the two extremes. And that is why the English Church assumed the form it still retains. Ritual, Prayer Book and the Thirty-Nine Articles were all framed to conciliate, as far as possible, both moderate Catholicism and moderate Protestantism.

The Church, then, was a National Church, no longer part of an international body. It was the Church *of* England, not the Church *in* England. But it was not a department of State. It was parallel with the State. At the head of both Church and State was the Crown. But whereas sovereignty in the State lay with the King in Parliament, sovereignty in the Church lay with the Crown alone, for the powers of the Pope had been transferred to the Crown alone. So to sum up this, the first stage in the long journey towards religious freedom, we may say that although there was now a national Church which had a monopoly, since no other Church was allowed, it was not yet controlled by the nation.

The Elizabethan settlement was a compromise—a very typical English compromise—and it was administered at first with, for those days, quite extraordinary moderation. The Queen had no desire, she said, "to open windows into her subjects' hearts". Unfortunately, religion is the subject on which people find it hardest to compromise. Even from the first it was difficult for a good Roman Catholic to be a loyal English subject. The Pope had refused to annul Henry's marriage to Katherine. Therefore, to a sound Papist Elizabeth was illegitimate. And when in 1570 the Pope actually excommunicated her and declared her subjects released from their allegiance, every Roman Catholic became a potential traitor.

Toleration was no longer possible. In 1571 it was enacted treason to join, or to persuade others to join, the Church of Rome, and later Acts proscribed the whole Catholic priesthood and savagely penalised any open manifestation of the Roman faith. In the last twenty-eight years of the reign, nearly two hundred persons were put to death. But remember that though these men were martyrs to their faith, they were also traitors to their country; and it was for their treachery, not for their faith, that they were condemned.

28

You see, England was in great danger. Europe was divided between Catholics and Protestants much as it is now divided between Fascism and Communism, with England holding a middle position in her religion then, as she does with her democracy to-day. The defeat of the Armada, in 1588, relaxed the tension. All danger of a Catholic restoration was really over. But who was to know that then? There were no statistics, no newspapers. And when, some time afterwards, the penal laws were more or less suspended, Catholics, who had conformed in order to escape the penalties, naturally showed themselves in their true colours again. It looked as though Popery were rapidly spreading. On top of that, in 1605, came Guy Fawkes's Gunpowder Plot. That threw the nation into a panic, and the penal laws of 1606 reached the high-water mark of anti-Catholic legislation.

These laws remained on the Statute Book. But they weren't strictly, regularly or even universally, enforced. Their bark was worse than their bite. They were like chained watch-dogs which could be let loose at the first signs of trouble.

Popery had been defeated as much by patriotism as by Protestantism. The Elizabethan religious compromise now had to face an attack from the other extreme—Calvinism. For the Calvinism of Geneva was the fighting doctrine of Protestantism and during

England's struggle with the Counter-Reformation had made great headway. There was no serious trouble till Elizabeth's death, for, as the Commons told James, they put up with a lot from her on account of her age and sex. But on James's accession the issue was fairly joined.

The Puritan movement, as it is called, began with objections to the traditional vestments of the clergy. From vestments the controversy spread to ritual, and from ritual to doctrine. And, since all these were enforced by the bishops, the Puritans were driven to attack the episcopal system. That was the crux of the matter. They didn't, as yet, want to *abolish* episcopacy; they wanted to modify episcopal autocracy. Every bishop should be assisted, they said, by a Synod—that is, an assembly of the clergy of his diocese. And James, who in his youth in Scotland had suffered endless humiliations from ministers of the Presbyterian kirk—they burst into his presence at all times and lectured him; they plucked him by the sleeve and called him "God's sillie vassal"— James, I say, summed up the whole situation perfectly in four words: "No Bishop; No King."

No Bishop; No King. He was right. A democratic Church was incompatible with an autocratic State. Admit democracy in the one, and you couldn't for long keep it out of the other. Agreement was impossible. Negotiations were broken off, and the only good that came of them was the Authorised Version of the Bible. On the other hand, three hundred clergy were deprived of their livings, left the Church and were followed by large congregations of sympathisers. The National Church, which had never included the Roman Catholics, was now losing its hold on the Protestants. James, and after him Charles, made matters worse by patronising a new High Church movement and trying to enforce it on the parishes. The Puritans, never very discreet in their language, grew noisier and ruder. Bishops, Priests and Deacons were described as "the little toes of Antichrist"; the clergy were "a generation of vipers...illiterate asses"; and the officials of the ecclesiastical courts were "filthy locusts that came out of the bottomless pit". The government replied with whippings, the pillory, mutilation, fines and imprisonment for life. Puritanical Parliaments grew more and more exasperated. The religious controversy tacked itself on to all the constitutional, financial and other questions at issue between King and Commons. And the result was rebellion and Civil War.

The Civil War was won neither by Church, nor King, nor Parliament, but by the Army. Church, King and Parliament all disappeared—abolished by a military dictatorship. But the Army proved a great

31

deal more tolerant than any of them, because it was composed of men of various sects. Three of these sects—Presbyterians, Independents and Baptists—became officially established and endowed, but any form of Protestant worship was tolerated publicly—provided the Prayer Book was not used. So under the Commonwealth the English had a first taste of limited Toleration. It rather went to their heads. But, in spite of the queer behaviour of a few hysterical fanatics, it did at least show that uniformity in religion was not as essential as had been supposed.

But it did not last. Army rule was never popular, and at Cromwell's death it collapsed. Church and King and Parliament were restored. But the Restoration Parliament was anything but tolerant. It contained all those who had suffered most during the interregnum, and they were out for revenge. They passed a series of laws, known as the Clarendon Code, which gave the Church a complete monopoly of preaching, teaching, publishing and public worship. And when the more liberal-minded Charles II attempted to suspend these laws, they capped them with the Test Act of 1673 by which the Holy Sacrament according to the rites of the Church became a test for every office in the State.

By the Clarendon Code two thousand clergy—one-fifth of the total number—were deprived of their livings, and something like the same proportion of the population were driven outside the pale of the Church. The claim of the Church to be National had become absurd. Its monopoly of worship was both absurd and cruel. And the Test Act made it a class Church—the Church of the official classes, of the gentry and their dependents, for the Puritan gentry, having too much to lose in political and social status, for the most part conformed. And, in spite of all the changes since, the Church still preserves traces of that characteristic to-day. I had a mild experience myself of it when serving with the Navy in the war. A sergeant of marines asked me what religion I would like to have initialled on my identity disc—and then, anxious no doubt to save a temporary officer from making a bloomer, he added: "I think most of the *gentlemen*, sir, prefer to be C.E."

The Restoration Church, buttressed by the Clarendon Code and the Test Act, seemed unassailable. As a matter of fact, it was already being betrayed from within—and from the most unlikely quarter— the Crown. The Crown had made the Church and was its head. The two had always supported each other. "For Church and King" is still a slogan of loyalty to-day.

But both Charles II and James II wanted to restore Catholicism. Charles, after burning his fingers badly, desisted. But nothing could teach brother James. He relied on a packed Parliament, on the Catholics, on the Protestant Dissenters, and on an army. They all let him down.

The revival of the Catholic menace once more drove all Protestants into one camp. Dissenters preferred Anglican persecution to Catholic toleration. Churchmen found it hard to go back on their cherished principle of passive obedience, but most of them did, and a bishop was one of the signatories to the letter inviting William of Orange to come over. He came. And all James's props and plans collapsed like a house of cards. The Revolution was as bloodless as it was successful.

The Revolution of 1688 marks the end of the second stage in the progress towards religious liberty. Nominally the Crown retained—as it still retains—its old supremacy over the Church, but actually Parliament was now supreme. Already, in 1664, the clergy had surrendered to Parliament their right to tax themselves separately in Convocation, and from 1717 onwards Convocations were to cease for over a century even to meet at all. But most significant of all was the clause in the Bill of Rights, passed immediately after the Revolution, by which Parliament insisted that in future the King must be a Protestant. The Church settlements of Henry VIII, Edward VI, Mary and

34

Elizabeth were all based on the principle that the subject must be of the same religion as his sovereign. Now that principle is reversed. In future the sovereign must be of the same religion as his subjects.

As for the Church itself, it still stood half-way between Rome and Geneva. It stands there still to-day. It has fought off the attacks of both. Yet both have left their mark. From the Catholics it has inherited and retains certain vestments and ritual, and from the Puritans it has picked up and adopted what has been called the Englishman's sad Sabbath. And although it has long ceased to be—in fact, it never was—the Church of the whole nation, it still remains the Established Church of the State.

All that is as true now as it was in 1689. But as regards religious liberty the situation then was very different. The Test Act remained in force, so Churchmen continued to enjoy their monopoly of all offices in the State. But they lost their monopoly of worship. That they had now to share with the Protestant Dissenter. The Dissenters, you see, had helped to make the Revolution. They had refused James's bribes. During the crisis, the Bishops had promised them toleration. William himself was a Calvinist, and there was danger of invasion by Catholic France. Some sort of toleration had to be granted. And the Toleration Act of 1689 did in effect grant freedom of worship to all but Catholics and Unitarians. You may think that didn't amount to much, and it is true that even that much was grudgingly granted, not on principle, but as a political necessity. But it did make a breach in the Church's stronghold of privilege. And the next stage of advance towards religious freedom consisted in widening that breach till the privileges of Churchmen had become the rights of all Englishmen.

It was a slow process—partly because the penal laws were so laxly enforced that they never precipitated a crisis. Dissenters who took office and failed to comply with the Test Act came to be protected by annual Acts of Indemnity. The more or less public worship of Catholics was winked at, and the worst laws against them lay dormant or were evaded. Conservatism preserved the law as it was, but custom modified its execution—a typically English procedure. Foreigners call it hypocrisy; we call it common sense.

But connivance at evasion was one thing, repeal another. Among the upper classes, the religious fervour of the seventeenth century had given way to the rationalism of the eighteenth. But the lower classes and the lesser clergy were by no means so tolerant. "The Church in Danger" was always a good cry to raise the mob with. Walpole, sympathetic as he was, could not throughout his long ministry be persuaded

36

to touch legal relief for Dissenters. He preferred, as he said, to let sleeping dogs lie. And, later on, the repeal in 1778 of a few provisions against Catholics provoked the worst riots in our history.

However, Parliament on that occasion stood firm and in 1791 went much further. Though it did not actually repeal, it nullified the effect of most of the penal laws against Catholics. And whereas, a century before, the Toleration Act had been regarded as a matter of expediency and the penal laws as a matter of principle, from now on toleration was accepted in principle and the exceptions to it defended only on grounds of expediency. Finally, by the repeal of the Test and Corporation Acts in 1828 and by the passage of the Catholic Emancipation Act in 1829, practically every office in the State was thrown open to Catholics and Dissenters alike on the same footing as members of the Established Church.

Religious liberty had come at last. But it had not come as a general principle. It was not uniform for all faiths. And it was not expressed in one law or code of laws. It had grown up haphazard, a bit at a time, and there remained therefore many anomalies to be cleared up. Nonconformists were, for instance, still obliged to be married in a parish church and to pay Church rates. They were also excluded from the Universities. And some sects—Quakers, Moravians,

37

Separatists and Unitarians—had in the past received exceptional treatment, favourable or adverse, from the State. All these required—and got—special legislation to bring them into line.

So did the Jews. They had always been on a different footing from anyone else. In the early Middle Ages they were the only inhabitants of England who were not members of the Church. They were hardly in any sense members of the State. They lived under special laws of their own at the mercy of the King, who protected them because he found them financially useful. But Edward I turned them out of the country and they were not allowed to return openly till the palmy days of toleration under the Commonwealth. The repeal of the Test and Corporation Acts brought them no relief, because they could not take the new oath "on the true faith of a Christian". And even after that difficulty had been removed they still could not enter Parliament, because the Parliamentary Oath was also "on the true faith of a Christian", and although from 1858 Lords and Commons allowed them to omit the awkward phrase, the oath itself was not legally altered until 1866.

The new oath, as amended two years later, concluded with the phrase "So help me God", and around these words was fought the last—or latest— famous battle for religious freedom. At the General

Election of 1880, Charles Bradlaugh, an outspoken Atheist, was returned for Northampton. He claimed the right to make an affirmation, instead of taking the oath. When that was refused, he offered to take the oath including what he called its "meaningless addendum". That too, was refused, and in the end he was allowed to affirm subject to the ruling of the Courts. The Courts decided against him and vacated his seat. He stood again, was re-elected and presented himself once more to take the oath. When the House repeatedly refused to let him do so, he produced a copy of the New Testament which he had brought with him and administered the oath to himself. He was promptly expelled, and a new writ was issued for Northampton. Re-elected again, he repeated the process. The Government now took proceedings against him and won their case. So he resigned his seat and was again elected with an increased majority. And when he was yet once more returned for North-ampton at the General Election of 1885, the House, having made a considerable fool of itself, at last gave way. Bradlaugh took the oath and his seat, and in 1888 an Act was passed allowing a solemn affirmation to be made on conscientious grounds instead of the oath.

There are still a few anomalies left, but they are so obscure, intricate and trivial that I don't think we need worry about them! Religious liberty in this country is pretty complete. We can profess any religion we like, or none. We can worship privately or publicly in any way we like, or not at all. And neither profession nor performance makes any difference to our civil or political rights—except that the King may not become or marry a Papist and a Roman Catholic cannot become Lord Chancellor. We may even, generally speaking, say and publish what we like about religion, provided we speak and write in good faith and in decent terms.

The Established Church has some privileges but also some disabilities. Thus, the bishops—or, rather, some of them—sit in the House of Lords. But no clergyman may sit in the House of Commons. Nor may Roman Catholic priests. But any Nonconformist minister may. The Church is not even master in its own house. Its dogma and ritual are fixed by law and may only be altered by Parliament. Quite recently the National Assembly of the Church passed a Measure to make certain alterations in the Prayer Book. But in 1927 and again in 1928 that Measure was rejected by Parliament, a large proportion of whose members were not members of the Church at all. That looks like an anomaly, doesn't it? But then some people regard an established Church as itself an anomaly. What do you think?

III

FREEDOM AND THE GOVERNMENT

Let me explain at once that I am dealing in this talk with the growth of our freedom in relation to *the* Government, that is, not Government in general, not *all* authority, but one particular authority, the King and his ministers, the Executive—as opposed to the Legislature which is Parliament, and the Judiciary which is the Courts of Law.

Not that our early Kings made any such distinction —any more than does the modern housewife. A mother lays down certain rules for her children, sees that they are carried out and punishes the child that breaks the rules. In doing so, she exercises legislative, executive and judicial functions. But she isn't aware of it, and I don't suppose she would be particularly grateful if you told her. So it was with the Kings of the Anglo-Norman period. They, too, performed all these functions in their Court.

And out of their Court grew, not only the Executive, but the whole of our constitution—except the House of Commons. And we need to know just enough about that process to be able to understand what happens to-day.

It will be easiest if we think of those early Kings as landlords. The King had tenants, each tenant had subtenants—and so on down to the smallest free-holder. And every important landowner, then as now, had servants and officials to help him run his estates. But, under the *feudal* system, every landlord *also* had *jurisdiction* over his tenants—that is, he had a Court, which his tenants had to attend.

Now the King's Court was like any other lord's Court, only more so. He, too, had his servants and officials—Steward, Chamberlain, Chancellor, Treasurer and so on; and he, too, had a Court which his tenants had to attend. He didn't always need them. Ordinary business could be done by his house-hold. But for important business he *would* need his more important tenants—or barons, as they came to be called—for their advice and backing in whatever he proposed to do. So you have to picture the King's Court as an elastic affair, which always included officials and might be reinforced by barons, few or many, according to the importance of the occasion.

Apart from being a landlord, the King's powers were at first very limited. The Church was part of an international organisation under the Pope; the barons had private jurisdiction over their lands and tenants, and the remoter parts of England were very wild and semi-independent. But he did have some advantages that other landlords hadn't. He was *nobody's* tenant. There was no Court above his. So he couldn't be legally called to account. That is what is meant by the phrase: "The King can do no wrong." It doesn't mean that he is perfect, but simply that there is no legal way of proceeding against him. Again, he was protected by a special law, the law of treason, which put him on a different footing from other men. And, above all, there was the Common Law. The Common Law was nothing more nor less than the custom of the country applied in Courts in every county before the Normans came over. To the King it was a godsend, because this National system of law could be used throughout the country to offset the feudal jurisdiction of the barons.

So by one means or another, the King gradually extended his authority. That put a lot more work on his Court. The work had to be parcelled out among individual officials and committees. So that, in time, instead of one King's Court there came to be many—the Courts of Law, the High Court of Parliament, and so on, all of which had grown out of the King's Court but were becoming independent bodies. The Constitution was being born.

But even so the King's Court—or Council as it was

now called—continued to be as busy as ever. The new institutions were not yet fully grown. They were still weak. They couldn't cope with everything. There were gaps to fill. And, besides, the King was still taking on new duties, as his power increased. In short, his business was expanding too rapidly for its organisation. So, to sum up the position at the end of the Middle Ages, we may say that, although Parliament and Courts of Law were already in existence, the King's Council still did, not only executive work, but a tremendous amount of supplementary judicial and legislative work as well.

The feudal overlord was becoming a national King, and the English people were beginning to feel themselves a nation. But national aspirations were blocked everywhere by the anti-national privileges and immunities of Church and baronage. And the barons chose this moment for a final bid for power. For a time they succeeded in getting control of the Council, and, through it, of the whole constitution. The result was chaos culminating in Civil War. But the Wars of the Roses themselves had two grand results—the extermination of most of the baronage and the accession of the Tudors. And the Tudors gave the country just what it wanted. Henry VII restored the rule of law and broke the power of the surviving barons. Henry VIII nationalised the Church, united

44

Wales with England and brought under control the semi-independent principalities of the North and West. And Elizabeth secured the country from foreign aggression.

All this was done without a standing army, a police force or a civil service. Parliament, of course, passed the necessary Acts and in this century won the experience that enabled it to challenge the Crown in the next. But it was the Council that had to carry the policy out. And the Tudor Council consisted of a handful of picked bureaucrats, most of them middle-class men, depending solely on the Crown for their advancement. This small body brought strong government into every corner of England, and where the Council itself could not reach, it employed the local gentry as Justices of the Peace to carry out its instructions in every village in England.

To get through this enormous task, the Council had to split itself up into a number of Courts and Committees, just as its predecessor the King's Court had done before in the old days. And these conciliar Courts—especially the Star Chamber—have been given a bad name in history, mainly because of their abuse later on under the Stuarts. But in Tudor times they were popular, because they gave quick, strong and impartial justice to rich and poor alike. And if all this administrative jurisdiction was often arbitrary

45

and sometimes tyrannical—even though it could be cruel, as in its use of torture, which the Common Law Courts never used—in spite of all that, it was tolerated gladly because at the time it was necessary. Sovereignty—absolute sovereignty—there had to be for the sake of order and national unity. In some countries, to-day, Fascism is defended on the same grounds. In sixteenth-century England, it was necessary that all the so-called "liberties" and privileges of the mediaeval Church and baronage should be sucked up into the sole power of the Crown, before they could begin to be distributed again, like rain, evenly throughout the land as the liberties of the people.

That explains why, for instance, Master Stubbe, the Puritan lawyer, when his right hand was struck off by the executioner, immediately snatched off his hat with his left and cried out: "Long live Queen Elizabeth!" And that is why Parliament, in granting taxes for the last time to the aged Queen, did so, they said: "Because no age hath nor can produce the like precedent of so much happiness under any prince's reign."

But despotism had served its purpose by then. The need for it had passed. Unfortunately Elizabeth was succeeded in 1603 by James I, a Scot, who did not understand our constitution. Foreigners seldom do. It works out so differently in practice from what it appears on paper. And James had a very good opinion of himself, both as a person and as King. "I am neither God nor an angel," he thought it necessary to tell his Council, "but a man like any other." But, as King, he was not like other men, he thought, because he believed in his Divine Right to rule.

The Divine Right of Kings, as a theory, was harmless enough. But in practice, among those who took it seriously, it did tend to exalt the royal power. And James took it very seriously. The judges made matters worse by trying to give a legal explanation for all the vague and undefined supplementary powers of the Crown with which we have just been dealing. The King's ordinary power, they said, was limited by Common Law; but, they added, he had in emergencies an absolute power, which was unlimited.

Now the English nation as a whole didn't care— and doesn't care—two hoots about theories and doctrines. At any given stage of our history, the feeling is that certain things *ought* to be done, and certain things ought *not* to be done. That is the English attitude. The Tudors hadn't bothered to bolster up their power with a theory. They just exercised it, and the nation tolerated it because it was necessary. Now it wasn't necessary. It was a nuisance. But the nuisance might have abated gradually and without fuss if the Stuarts hadn't dug themselves in with theory and so made compromise impossible.

In less than forty years, through sheer tactlessness, James I and Charles I succeeded in alienating every section of the nation. A straight fight developed between the Common Law, in which our freedom was embedded, and Prerogative, which was the fortress of despotism.

But the King still held the trump card. Opposition could only come from Parliament, and only the King could summon Parliament. He could also dismiss it as soon as he liked. He could even do without it at a pinch. Charles did for eleven years, and was getting on quite nicely, when he committed an act of appalling folly which destroyed him.

He tried to force an episcopalian Prayer Book on the presbyterian Scots. The Scots invaded England. Charles could not turn them out. They demanded an indemnity. Only Parliament could raise the money, so Parliament had to be summoned. And, as the Scots refused to go home till they were paid, the King could not dismiss Parliament till the money was voted. And, before it voted the money, Parliament made itself secure. It passed an Act by which it could only be dissolved with its own consent. And then proceeded at leisure to abolish the Star Chamber and other Courts of the Council and to deprive the Crown of all the supplementary powers, legislative and judicial, that it had possessed and developed since time immemorial.

Now that upset the centre of gravity of English government. The two rivals for power were the King and Parliament. Up till now, owing to the extraordinary powers developed by the Council, the King had been boss. Those extraordinary powers had just been abolished. Who would now be boss? King, or Parliament? the Executive, or the Legislature? Most people at the time thought that neither should be boss, but that each should be independent in its own sphere. But suppose the King had one policy and Parliament another? There would be a deadlock. And that is exactly what happened with Charles and the Long Parliament. He had one policy; it had another. There came a deadlock, and, since neither would give way, there was a Civil War.

The Civil War left the matter unsettled, because it was won by neither King nor Parliament, but by Cromwell's army. The Restoration left it unsettled, because the nation was so glad to get its King and constitution back that it did not worry about the terms. The same sort of deadlock recurred in the reign of James II, and the result was a Revolution, but this time no bloodshed.

Now, you'd expect, wouldn't you, that after nearly a century of domestic commotion, there would be some sort of constitutional spring-cleaning. At least you'd think they would settle this fundamental issue of the relationship between Executive and Legislature once and for all. But no. It was taken for granted that the constitution was all right, only James had violated it. Therefore all that was necessary, and all that was done, was to enumerate in a Bill of Rights certain practices of his and condemn them.

Other things resulted incidentally. For instance, by conferring the Crown on William and Mary, Parliament broke the line of the succession. That *incidentally* killed Divine Right. And the fact that, whereas half the nation had sided with Charles I, not a soul would fight for James II, showed *incidentally* that, if it came to a show-down, the Legislature could be sure of beating the Executive. But you couldn't afford to have a Revolution every time the Executive fell out with the Legislature. And yet what else could you do? The King was the active head of the Executive—his own Prime Minister, as we should say—and there was no *legal* way of calling him to account. And it was difficult to make ministers responsible, apart from the King, because what they did was done by his orders. They were appointed and dismissed by him. They carried out his policy. To sum up, as long as the King controlled policy, ministerial responsibility was difficult to enforce.

Once again—as so often in our history—we failed to invent a remedy. The problem was solved in the end by the evolution of the Cabinet, the Prime Minister and Party Government. But we can't be said to have invented any of them. They grew up, typically enough, in spite of us. All three were bitterly resented, and every effort was made to stifle their development. The Cabinet was regarded as secret and sinister; parties were thought factious and disloyal, and, even as late as 1806, it could still be said in Parliament that "the Constitution abhors the idea of a Prime Minister".

The Cabinet began in this way. In Tudor times, the executive part of the Council's work was done by a small and efficient inner ring of officials, called the Privy Council. The Stuarts enlarged it with a lot of decorative, but unnecessary, favourites, noblemen and bishops, till it became too large to discuss policy as one body and had to be split up into committees. The King couldn't attend all these committees, but only the most important. So one of these, the Foreign Committee, came in time, for convenience, to be composed of all the most important councillors, and all important questions of policy were discussed there. The popular name for this small and secret body had always been the "cabal" or "cabinet", and the latter name eventually stuck. By Queen Anne's time, the Cabinet, in spite of all efforts to abolish it as a usurper, had become the recognised Executive, while the Privy Council, of which the Cabinet was supposed to be a committee, had become a purely formal body, as it is to-day. A wit summed up the change neatly in 1711: "The Privy Councillors", he said, "were such as were thought to know everything and knew nothing. Those of the Cabinet Council thought nobody knew anything but themselves."

The Prime Minister grew out of the Cabinet. George I, who succeeded Anne, was a German and knew no English. He therefore gave up attending meetings of the Cabinet. Someone had to preside in his place and act as link between Cabinet and King. Hence the Prime Minister. Walpole was really the first one, though he always denied it—as did his successors. You see, the title was still a term of abuse, borrowed from the French and suggestive of arbitrary government. All ministers, it was still felt, were equally the King's servants, severally responsible for their individual departments, and it was a long time before the predominance of a single minister over his colleagues ceased to be regarded as unconstitutional. The younger Pitt consolidated the position in his long administration at the end of the eighteenth century. But it took another generation to perfect the principles of Cabinet solidarity and unanimity in public. Lord Melbourne, who was Prime Minister on Queen Victoria's accession, summed up these principles with unconscious humour, when he called upstairs to his colleagues one day after a Cabinet dinner: "Well, what are we going to say about this? Are we going to raise the price of corn, or lower it, or keep it steady? I don't care what we say, but we'd better all say the same thing."

But the growth of the Cabinet and Prime Minister did not of themselves, of course, make ministers responsible to Parliament. That was the work of political parties. The first real party split occurred just before the Civil War began in Charles I's reign, between those who afterwards fought for the King and those who fought against him. But the origin of the two great historical parties, Whig and Tory, dates from the constitutional struggles of Charles II's reign. The King's power of choosing his ministers was still unfettered, but these ministers had to face Parliament, and it soon became difficult to keep ministers in power, if they did not belong to the party which had a majority in the House of Commons.

For a time the King held his own, because he possessed enormous patronage which he could distribute among members in exchange for support of his government. He was thus able to create an artificial majority for his ministers. But that patronage was gradually abolished by statute, and the passing of the Reform Act of 1832 made artificial majorities impossible. The franchise now was much more widely distributed, constituencies could no longer be bought and sold, and the electorate returned candidates pledged to support one or other of the parties. The majority party in the House would naturally only support ministers chosen from its own members, and without that support government could not be carried on. So the King's choice of ministers was no longer free. In practice he had to appoint as Prime Minister the acknowledged leader of the majority party, and let the Prime Minister choose the rest of the ministry. In short, the control of the Executive had passed from Crown to Parliament.

The House of Commons, then, controls the Cabinet. But wait a moment. It would be just as true to say that the Cabinet controls the House of Commons. In theory any member of the Commons can initiate legislation; in practice nearly all legislation is initiated by the Cabinet. The Cabinet decides beforehand what laws it will promote, and it promotes so many that little time is left for the bills or motions of private members. The Cabinet has to watch the pulse of the House and especially of its own majority, and, if its

54

majority is small, it must watch its step as well. But party discipline is strict, and when the majority is a large one, it is hardly too much to say that the Cabinet legislates with the automatic consent of the House of Commons.

Mind you, I don't say that our freedom is much the worse for that. If the Cabinet dominates the House of Commons, it shows an increasing sensitiveness to public opinion outside. That sensitiveness has become more and more marked with every extension of the franchise, as is only natural; for, the more complete the democracy, the greater the influence of public opinion. For instance, since the Reform Act of 1867, governments when defeated at a General Election have resigned at once, without waiting for the verdict of the House of Commons. Party organizations have sprung up through which the leaders of the various parties keep in touch with opinion in the constituencies. And in their public utterances, both inside and outside the House, ministers are usually more concerned to convince the public than the House of Commons. Even foreign politics, which until the war anyway were a very hush-hush business conducted by secret diplomacy, may now be directly modified by public opinion—instance the recent resignation of Sir Samuel Hoare. We hear complaints sometimes that ministers are usurping the functions of diplomats.

If they do so, isn't it, perhaps, because ministers are more in touch with, and responsible to, public opinion, and democracy will not be left out?

But this matter of the Cabinet's control over the Commons, and so over Parliament, is only part of a much wider problem—the tremendous powers of the Executive in this country to-day *outside the Executive sphere*. The function of an Executive is administration. But our Executive does much more than that. And we ought to know what and why.

The explanation lies in our history, and that is why I have tried to trace in this talk the evolution of our present-day Executive out of the old King's Court of Anglo-Norman times. That King's Court, we saw, performed all the functions of government—executive, legislative and judicial; and the King's Council, which descended from it, continued to do so in a supplementary way, even after Parliament and the Courts of Law were fully grown, until the Long Parliament abolished all the Courts of the Council and destroyed practically all its legislative and judicial powers. From then on we should expect the Privy Council, and later its offspring the Cabinet, to be a purely executive body without any legislative or judicial functions whatever.

But that is not true, because our Executive, like every other portion of our constitution, retains traces of its historical origin. We never went in for a complete "separation of powers" as it is called—in other words, a complete divorce between Executive, Legislature and Judiciary. Other countries have done so, notably the U.S.A., but we haven't. With us they are still mixed up—or, at least, they overlap. To take only one instance, the members of our Executive, the Cabinet, are also members of the Legislature, Parliament; and the Lord Chancellor, who is invariably a member of the Cabinet, is invariably also the presiding officer of the House of Lords and also the head of our Judiciary.

That, you may say, is merely a quaint historical survival. But it explains why and how the government is able to perform other than executive duties. The presence of the government in Parliament has in conjunction with other things I have dealt with—namely, the evolution of a Prime Minister, of Cabinet solidarity, ministerial responsibility and the extension of the franchise—all these together have brought about a situation which enables the Executive to control practically all Parliamentary legislation.

But what it doesn't explain is a recent phenomenon, which may have—indeed, already has—serious consequences to our liberty. Apart from its powers of legislation *in* Parliament, the Executive has begun to develop very real powers, both legislative and

57

judicial, *outside* Parliament. Our overworked Parliament tends to pass more and more of its legislation in skeleton form, at the same time authorising the ministry to fill in the gaps with Regulations and to apply these Regulations itself in individual cases. About this new administrative law, and its Star Chamber qualities, I shall have more to say in connexion with Freedom and the Law. But you will find it all authoritatively dealt with by Lord Chief Justice Hewart in his book *The New Despotism*.

And finally, one word of warning. In this talk, I have been mainly concerned with the *history* of the Executive and the *growth* of our freedom in relation to it. But when we come to examine our liberty in relation to other institutions and analyse it as it is to-day, we shall find that, when our freedom has been threatened, the offender, more often than not, has been the Executive. You see, all through the sixteenth century and half the seventeenth, it was the all-powerful instrument of despotism. It took first a Rebellion and then a Revolution to put it back in its proper place. In the eighteenth century (as we shall see when we come to deal with Parliament) it built up its power again on bribery and corruption. And after being momentarily checked in the first half of the nineteenth century, here it is in the twentieth perking up again.

Don't misunderstand me. I know that strong government in a democracy is absolutely vital. Recent events abroad have proved that over and over again. But the Executive is not merely the Cabinet. In its wider sense it includes the civil service and the police. And a too powerful bureaucracy is as fatal to democratic freedom as weak government. It stifles it with regimentation.

In fact, I don't know which is worse. The Executive that doesn't do its job, or the one that overdoes it. Let me give you an example of each.

Recently, a lady I know went to a big political meeting. After about twenty minutes, a rough house started near her. She managed to get clear and reached the door. In the lobby was a policeman. He referred her to the Inspector. She found the Inspector, told him what was happening and asked him to stop it. He said: "We have our orders." "But surely," she insisted, "you are here to keep order!" "No," replied the Inspector.

Here's an instance of the other extreme. It happened in Berlin in 1909. Roller-skating had just come in, and as the streets were asphalt, we—that's a German friend and myself—thought we'd go about on skates. We got as far as the Brandenburger Tor, right in the middle of the town, when a very smart policeman came out of a police station and stopped us. "Take those things off," he ordered. "Why?" we asked. "They're forbidden," he said. "They can't be forbidden," protested my friend, who was older and braver than me, "they've only just been invented."

That puzzled him. He fetched out a superior policeman, whose gold braid and brass glittered like a Christmas tree. The same conversation took place. Then he, too, retired and returned with a perfectly terrific policeman. But he couldn't solve the problem. He invited us inside. I was terrified. Well, we waited about twenty minutes, while they sent for someone grander still. When he came, he was so grand that he didn't even wear uniform. He had a top hat and frock coat instead. They put the problem to him. "But isn't it true, they aren't forbidden?" burst in my friend impetuously. The Great Man twirled his moustache. "Boys," he said at last, gently but firmly, "everything is forbidden unless it is expressly allowed."

We took off our skates.

Well, we haven't got as far as that yet. But there's no knowing.

IV

FREEDOM AND THE FORCES

I ENDED up my last talk by pointing out the Executive as the Big Bad Wolf in the history of our Freedom. So it proved in the history of our armed forces, as long as they were solely under Executive control. The Navy was less feared than the Army, because in the nature of things it couldn't be used to overawe the populace, but in more ways than one, it was made the excuse for interfering with our liberties.

Geography made the Navy. Until the discovery of America, the western world came to an end with the Atlantic seaboard. There was nothing farther west than the west of Europe. Trade, therefore, flowed eastward, and its maritime highway was the Mediterranean. England, far away off the North-West coast of Europe, was about as badly placed as it could be. There was a certain amount of trade north and south between the Mediterranean and the Baltic, but even that was mostly in foreign hands. Our main business at sea was not trade at all, but fishing.

But from the moment America was discovered, the tide of trade began to turn more and more definitely out of the Mediterranean into the Atlantic. And England was right on top of the Atlantic. Her chance had come.

We couldn't take advantage of it at once. We were too poor for one thing and only just recovering from the Wars of the Roses. On top of that we had the religious upsets of the Reformation. By the time we were ready to exploit this brave New World, the Spaniards and Portuguese had divided it between them. But Spain and Portugal were too greedy; they had bitten off more than they could chew; and their power collapsed from sheer indigestion as quickly as it had swollen. Whereas we, forced by circumstances to go slow, laid humble but very solid foundations for a more gradual expansion.

It is to Henry VIII more than to any other single individual that we owe our Navy. Till then, there wasn't one. War at sea was fought with merchantmen. Merchantmen, you see, were armed even in peacetime because the seas were infested with pirates. Kings had a few ships of their own—a very few. They were exactly like other merchant ships, except that they had large superstructures fore and aft to accommodate armed men. In peacetime they were hired out to merchants; in wartime they acted as flagships.

But Henry VIII inherited a fortune from his father; and, later on, when he closed the monasteries, he made a packet out of the sale of their lands. He indulged in an orgy of warship construction. Both in design and in armament he adopted new principles which were not radically altered till the nineteenth century. What's more, he built and equipped dock-yards; and, most important of all, by instituting the Navy Board, he created a permanent organisation ashore for naval supplies. As a result of his programme —probably the most extensive ever carried out in this country—we possessed a Navy second to none.

Our maritime policy thenceforward developed along three main lines: First, the control of the narrow seas and the protection of our shores from invasion; secondly, the expansion of trade; and, thirdly, the acquisition of colonies.

To control the narrow seas we had to fight Spain in the sixteenth century (for Spain then held what is now Belgium), the Dutch in the seventeenth, the French in the eighteenth, and the Germans in the twentieth. Trade was encouraged because it increased national wealth and still more because, for a long time to come, the fleet depended in war on mer-chant auxiliaries. So Navigation Acts were passed to secure for us the carrying trade to these shores; bounties were offered to private builders of large ships; and the eating of meat on certain days of the week was forbidden, even after the Reformation, in order to foster the fishing industry which trained the bulk of our seamen. Colonial expansion didn't come till later. Elizabeth thought the English would make bad colonists, because of what she called their "extreme beastly idleness".[1] For the time being we confined ourselves to smash and grab raids on other peoples' colonies.

You remember the old Jingo rhyme: "We've got the ships; we've got the men; we've got the money, too." Well, in those days, we had got the ships, but we hadn't got the money, and we were always short of men. It was in trying to get money and men that the Navy fell foul of the liberties of the subject.

In Tudor times, many naval undertakings—even some of Drake's most famous exploits—were financed by private syndicates, much in the same way as nowadays rich men and enterprising firms put up money for an air race or an attempt on a speed record. But in the end, of course, the nation's Navy had to be paid for by the nation. There lay the trouble. The nation thought it grand to have a Navy, but it didn't want to pay for it. Some politicians recently took much the same line with regard to our present re-armament. It was necessary—granted—but they

[1] Tunstall, *The Realities of Naval History*, p. 48.

64

weren't going to vote for it. There was more excuse in those days, perhaps, for adopting this attitude. Parliament did not yet control expenditure, so it could never be sure that the money would be spent on what it was voted for. Anyway, Charles I couldn't get on with his Parliaments. So he tried to raise the money without Parliament by reviving a very ancient and long obsolete custom. In Anglo-Saxon times, the country had been obliged to contribute by districts, either ships, or money in lieu of ships. That was six hundred years ago by then. So naturally, when Charles tried it on, many refused to pay. They were put in prison. There followed a first-class constitutional row on the principle of no taxation without Parliamentary consent, and ship money was one of the many grievances that brought about the Rebellion.

The Rebellion ended in a military dictatorship, and Cromwell, being a dictator, got all the money he wanted. He completed very thoroughly the work begun by Henry VIII. His policy was continued at the Restoration by Charles II and that famous Secretary to the Admiralty, Samuel Pepys. And we may date the modern Royal Navy in status, administration and finance from that time.

But there still remained the problem of personnel. Manning the fleet had always been a problem. In the eighteenth century it became critical. That was the period of our greatest expansion. There were constant wars and constant threats of invasion. Voluntary enlistment met with no response. And no wonder. The conditions of service were terrible. Pay was always months in arrears; food in those days could not be properly preserved at sea; the water was often stale or foul; punishments even for small offences were unbelievably brutal; and men went without shore leave sometimes for years.

The only way to get recruits was by pressing them, that is, by taking them by force. It was an ancient practice, based on immemorial custom, and, however disgraceful, it was undoubtedly legal. What happened was this. A naval officer, armed with a press-warrant, took up his quarters in a town, hung a Union Jack out of the window, hired a gang of toughs, and proceeded to waylay and forcibly seize as many men as he could. He was supposed only to take seamen, but in times of national emergency nobody was safe. Press-gangs even took to the water, waylaid ships returning from overseas, and pressed the unfortunate deckhands before they even set foot on shore.

Men enlisted in this way were little better than slaves. The system was tolerated on the grounds of national necessity. But it injured trade, since merchantmen were robbed of their crews; it infuriated the sea-coast population and led to innumerable riots; and it was an outrageously expensive method of obtaining recruits. Nelson estimated the cost at £20 a head. It could not fail in the end to demoralise the fleet.

At the end of the eighteenth century, in the middle of a war with France, matters came to a head. The men petitioned the Commander-in-Chief. Some of their petitions are very moving. Here is an extract from one of them:

"As for English Tars to be the Legitimate Sons of Liberty, it is an Old Cry which we have Experienced and Knows it to be False. God knows, the Constitution is admirable well Callculated for the Safety and Happiness of His Majesty's Subjects who live by Employments on Shore; but alass, we are not Considered as Subjects of the same Sovereign, unless it be to Drag us by Force from our Families to Fight the Battles of a Country which Refuses us Protection."[1]

To these petitions they got no answer. As a last resort they mutinied. On April 16th, 1797, the Channel Fleet refused to put to sea. The men offered no violence to their officers and scrupulously performed all other duties; but they would not raise the anchors till their grievances were redressed. And their demands were extremely moderate. In fact, the astonishing thing about this and other mutinies

[1] Hutchinson, *The Press-Gang*, p. 17.

that broke out elsewhere in sympathy is the dignity and restraint with which these ill-used men behaved. In the end their demands were conceded, and the battles of Camperdown, the Nile, Copenhagen and Trafalgar are sufficient evidence of the morale of the fleet. With the conclusion of peace in 1815, the need for press-gangs disappeared, and they were abolished by statute in 1833.

Since then the Navy has not interfered with our individual freedom, but it has continued to protect our collective freedom, our trade and our Empire from foreign aggression. It has done good work, too, for the freedom of other than British subjects. It took the lion's share in the abolition of the Slave Trade and thus atoned to some extent for the large share we had taken in that trade in the old days. It suppressed slavery ashore on the coasts of Africa and Asia. The Spanish and Portuguese colonies of South America, and Greece, too, owe their independence, in part at least, to our Navy; and quite recently it has rescued thousands of refugees from Spain.

Only in one way, I think, did the Navy infringe the liberty of other nations. Our supremacy at sea led naturally to the blockade of enemy harbours, to the searching of merchantmen at sea, to the confiscation of contraband, and to a general restraint of neutral trade in wartime. We were inclined to interpret the Freedom of the Seas as being our own private privilege. "Hence", to quote *1066 and All That*, "the important International Law called the Rule Britannia, technically known as the Freedom of the Seas."[1] Anyway, we made ourselves very unpopular. In the American War of Independence almost the whole of maritime Europe took advantage of our preoccupation to try and get their own back, either by active hostilities, or by armed neutrality against us.

More recently we seem to have learnt our lesson. In the Great War it was maddening to have to let pass such quantities of raw materials for war destined for Germany in neutral ships. But moderation paid in the end. And it was Germany's declaration of an unrestricted submarine blockade that brought the United States into the war on our side.

Just as there was no permanent Navy to start with, so there was no permanent Army. But whereas the Navy soon became popular, the Army till comparatively recently was loathed. The popularity of the Navy was due to geography. The unpopularity of the Army was due to history.

After the Conquest, the King had two kinds of military force at his disposal in wartime. First, there was the Feudal Levy. Every tenant owed military

[1] p. 11.

service to the Crown. He had to supply so many armed knights. But the feudal levy wasn't very satisfactory. It wasn't always loyal; it only had to serve for forty days a year; and it often made a fuss when ordered abroad. The King soon preferred to take a money payment instead.

Secondly, there was the National Levy. That dated from Anglo-Saxon times. Every freeman was liable and had to supply his own weapon. But he needn't serve outside his own county unless the country was invaded. So the King preferred to call up just a quota from each county and pay them himself. Notice that this amounted to conscription. It was legal. It probably still is. Anyway the right has never been abolished.

But far better than feudal or national levies, of course, were hired mercenaries—if you could afford them. You knew where you were with *them*. They were always foreigners at first, because there weren't any professional soldiers in England. But they were hated—naturally—and the King had to give them up. Instead, he took to hiring the retainers of great barons. But these in peacetime got out of hand and indulged in private warfare under their lords. After the Wars of the Roses they were suppressed.

So the Tudors in peacetime had nothing but a bodyguard of Beefeaters—the Yeoman of the Guard who still decorate the Tower of London. In wartime they raised a sort of cocktail army, composed of a feudal element, a conscript element from the national levy, and volunteers.

By Stuart times it was distinctly odd even for an island nation not to have a standing army. So anyway thought James I. He tried to insinuate the thin end of the wedge by not disbanding his troops when hostilities ceased. That led to all sorts of trouble. The troops had to be paid, and Parliament wouldn't pay them—it feared the troops might be used against itself. There were no barracks, so the troops had to be billeted on private houses. They had no discipline, because, according to the law of the land, soldiers in peacetime were ordinary citizens and subject only to the Common Law, and their riotous behaviour shocked a Puritan nation. James tried to remedy that by issuing commissions of martial law to govern not only the troops, but the civilians who came in contact with them as well. That was illegal, and in 1628 it was declared so.

But in the end it came to Civil War, and the Civil War revealed on both sides the inefficiency of the old-fashioned fighting machine. Then Cromwell raised a new army on a proper basis, knocked out all comers and proceeded with its support to rule the country till his death. That was the beginning of the

71

modern army, and it was hated as the instrument of arbitrary dictatorship.

At the Restoration it was disbanded, but Charles II managed to keep 5000 troops—the Coldstream Guards; and James II, on the strength of a rebellion that broke out on his accession, had as many as 15,000. He relied on them to enforce his illegal attempts to restore Roman Catholicism. But when the Revolution came, they refused to fight for him.

A standing army had become the symbol of tyranny. Yet what with the danger of Jacobite invasions and wars with France, a standing army there had to be. How to reconcile a standing army with liberty—that was the problem. It was solved in a typically English round-about way. The Bill of Rights of 1689 declared a standing army in time of peace to be illegal, except by consent of Parliament. But it became the practice—and it still is the practice —to pass an Act every year authorising the maintenance of a certain number of troops and a code of rules for their government—for one year only. By this means Parliament got and still has annual control of the number, cost and discipline of the Army.

Constant wars and rumours of wars soon got the nation accustomed to a standing army. But they didn't make it popular. By the end of the eighteenth century, officers were all right for young ladies to flirt with, as we know from Jane Austen's novels. But it wasn't till Victorian times that privates became nice for nursery-maids to know. You see, soldiers, like sailors, had to be enlisted by other than voluntary methods. Debtors, disorderly persons and even criminals were released from gaol provided they joined up. The British Army of the eighteenth century was largely composed of bad characters.

In the nineteenth century conditions improved, and voluntary enlistment produced enough men. In fact, there were plenty left over for the Militia, the Yeomanry and the Volunteers, as well—or, as they became in 1907, the Special Reserve and the Territorial Force. But, then, most of our nineteenth-century wars were small colonial affairs, or too remote to hit the nation hard. Even the Crimean War was a professional affair; even the Boer War was a long way off and took only a small proportion of our manhood. It seems odd when you think of it, but the nation as a whole never really learnt what war meant till 1914.

The Napoleonic Wars, you would think, were sufficiently a matter of life and death to us. But in the novels of Jane Austen, who lived and wrote throughout them, we meet plenty of officers, but hardly a mention of the war. A century passed before we came up against anything on the same scale, and when it did come, none of us realised its significance. I remember being absolutely amazed when Kitchener asked for one hundred thousand men. We all thought it would be over in three months, or at latest by Christmas. How abysmal our ignorance was I can illustrate by something I overheard on the 5th of August 1914—the day after we entered the war. I was riding home on top of a bus. There was a man, about 45, and a boy, about 12, sitting just in front of me. "What's a German, Daddy?" asked the boy. "No need to worry about them, George," answered his father. "We'll sink 'em with our searchlights."

Well, we learnt our lesson—at a price, and a part of the price was conscription. Two things puzzled me about that conscription. Let me put them to *you*. The Compulsory Service Act of 1916 exempted conscientious objectors. I came home on leave to hear quite accidentally that a friend of mine was about to appear before a tribunal as a "conshie". I volunteered to give evidence for him. As we waited his turn, I heard some dozen other cases being dealt with at the rate of about one to every five minutes. I was horror-struck at the stupidity and callousness of the butchers and bakers and candlestick-makers who sat on the bench. I was so hot and bothered that I went out of my way (I was very young at the

74

time) to get into touch with some other young men who, I heard, were about to plead conscientious objections. I saw something of them and, rightly or wrongly, came away with the impression that they were one and all of them bogus.

The point is this: If you're going to have conscription—and in a modern war how can you avoid it?—is there any value in a clause exempting conscientious objectors? To my mind, the martyr to *any* decent cause is a hero—whether it be his country's cause or conscientious objection to war. But how in the atmosphere of wartime will you ever get an impartial tribunal on the one hand, or distinguish the foxes from the lambs on the other? Freedom can't breathe in war.

My other problem was this. There was a great outcry at the time from certain quarters that conscription for the Army would lead to industrial conscription. Well, I may be very stupid, but why the dickens shouldn't it? If one man may be compelled to fight for his country, mayn't another man be compelled to work for it. I leave it to you.

There's another matter concerning Freedom and the Forces to be cleared up. We often hear of martial law and military law and court martials. Sometimes they seem to concern only soldiers, sometimes civilians are concerned as well. What is it all about?

Well, first of all let's get rid of a verbal confusion. Military law is properly speaking the special code of law that governs the soldier; martial law, in *this* country, is the assumption by the Crown of absolute power to suppress by force invasion or disorder.

In some countries—France, for instance—in certain circumstances a state of siege can be declared. Constitutional guarantees are thereby suspended, and the authority of the civil power becomes vested entirely in the Army. Martial law in this sense doesn't exist in England. It is illegal. But in *another* sense martial law does exist. For the Crown and its servants have a Common Law right to repel force with force in case of invasion, insurrection, riot, or violent breach of the peace. This right is not specially connected with the Army. It is the legal right and duty of *every* subject, whether civilian, policeman or soldier, to assist in putting down breaches of the peace, though obviously policemen and soldiers are by their profession best suited to the purpose. Martial law in this sense is on all fours with the right of every individual to protect his person and his property from the violence of others. Thus, no unnecessary force may be used, and the use of force must cease as soon as the need for it has ceased. And afterwards—and herein lies the main difference between our martial law and the continental variety—*afterwards*, soldiers,

76

policemen and civilians are equally accountable to the law for what they have done. And judges may decide whether the occasion justified the use of force, whether the amount of force used was or was not excessive, and whether or not the use of it stopped as soon as it should.

For over 300 years there has, I believe, been no proclamation of martial law in this country—though there has been in Ireland and in the colonies. Anyway such proclamation has no *legal* effect. It is merely a warning that a necessity has arisen for the use of force. It doesn't make the use of force any more legal, nor render those who use it any less accountable for their actions.

Now that is the law and has been for centuries. But in the old days it was not always observed. For instance, we saw how James I used so-called martial law to keep his troops in order, and even civilians associating with them, when he began to keep a standing army in peacetime. That martial law was declared illegal by the Petition of Right in 1628. The country didn't approve of an army in peacetime. The King had control of it and he might, it was thought, use it to suppress the liberties of the people. So there were no legal rules for military discipline till the Revolution, when in a roundabout way, which I have already described, Parliament got

77

control of the Army. Then at last it consented by
annual Mutiny Acts to authorise a special code of
rules for the better government of the Army. And that
was the beginning of our military law to which all
soldiers are subject.

But though a soldier is subject to military law, he
still remains subject also to Common Law. As a
member of the Army, he incurs special liabilities and
special duties. He can be punished for certain actions
which a civilian can commit with impunity; and for
other actions he can be punished more severely than
a civilian can be. He can be tried by Court Martial;
and in many ways he enjoys less freedom than a
civilian.

But he remains a citizen, and as a citizen he can
be tried in the Courts of Common Law as well. If
acquitted at Common Law, he can't be tried for the
same offence by Court Martial. On the other hand,
if acquitted by a Court Martial, he *can* be tried for
the same offence at Common Law. Again, a soldier
is bound to obey any lawful order of his superior
officer. But if he does anything illegal, he is liable
at Common Law, even though he was ordered to do
it by a superior officer. In theory, at any rate, his
position is not an enviable one. He may, as someone
has said, be shot by a Court Martial if he disobeys
an order, and hanged by judge and jury if he obeys

it. In actual practice obedience to an order is held to exonerate him unless the order was *obviously* illegal.

The soldier, then, has less freedom and greater liabilities than the ordinary citizen. Is he, then, a free man. I think the answer must be yes. Enlistment is a civil contract voluntarily entered into before a magistrate. Surely a soldier's status may be compared with that of a clergyman of the Established Church. He, too, undertakes special duties, is subject to special restrictions and special Courts, yet still remains amenable to the ordinary law of the land.[1]

And lastly, the subject of Freedom and the Forces raises a still wider question—too wide for me to deal with. I will pass it on to you. It is arguable—it has often been argued—that Army and Navy and Air Force—all of them curtail our liberty, because the money spent on them could be better spent, say, on the social services, where it would add to the sum of our social freedom. That argument, I suppose, is at the back of the minds of all who oppose our present rearmament. Well, the issue is clear. The risk of the total loss of our freedom lies in one scale; the certainty (if that risk does not materialise) of some gain in our social freedom lies in the other. We all pay our money, and we can all take our choice. Choose.

[1] Cf. Dicey, *The Law of the Constitution.*

79

V

FREEDOM AND THE LAW

FREEDOM in relation to the Law in this country has two aspects. It implies, first, that there is one system of law for all citizens, administered in independent Courts; and, secondly, that the laws are consistent with freedom and the processes of law protect that freedom.

Now the second of these two aspects belongs properly to a later stage in these talks when we come to discuss how our freedom works in practice to-day.[1] It is with the first aspect only that I am concerned in this talk.

In this country there is one system of law for all citizens called the Common Law, and it is applied by Judges, assisted sometimes by Juries. It is also applied by Magistrates, but we will leave them till later.[1] Common Law, Judges and Juries—these are our immediate concern.

Before the Conquest, every county had its Court, and so did the subdivisions of each county, called

[1] See Talk IX, *Freedom and Justice*.

Hundreds, and the law administered in these Courts was Customary Law—the custom of the country. The system of law which the Normans used was the feudal system, but the Anglo-Norman Kings were quick to see the usefulness of this national customary law as an offset to the private, feudal jurisdiction of the barons. They made the most of it; they tied it to the King's Court by sending justices periodically on tour to hear cases in the County Courts; and finally centralised the system by setting up three permanent Courts at Westminster. Thus the Customary Law of the Country became the Common Law, and the Common Law continued to expand. The judges expanded it, *naturally*, by interpreting it to meet each new case that came before them, and Parliament expanded it, *artificially*, by making new laws.

By the end of the Middle Ages it was a fairly comprehensive system of law. But it was by no means the only system of law. The Church had its Canon Law, the barons had their feudal jurisdiction, and the remoter parts of England were practically outside the general organisation of the kingdom. By the end of Henry VIII's reign, the Church had been nationalised, the country unified and the feudal jurisdictions practically destroyed. But in the process the royal prerogative had built up a new rival, the King's own Administrative Law, as practised in the Star Chamber and other Courts of the now all-powerful Council. These Courts we saw were eventually abolished by the Long Parliament in 1641.

But that wasn't the end. In this country institutions grow, decay and are sometimes destroyed, but nearly always there are a few tag-ends left over. About the insignificant remnants I needn't bother you, but there did survive one important system of law, called Equity, which I haven't yet mentioned.

Equity was the name for the rules of law applied by the Chancellor in the Court of Chancery. The King's Council in old days had exercised civil as well as criminal jurisdiction. The criminal jurisdiction developed in the Star Chamber, its civil jurisdiction developed in Chancery.

The Chancellor in early days was the head of the Royal Secretariat. People kept on coming to the King's Court with petitions of all sorts and were referred to the Chancellor. Whenever possible he packed them off with writs addressed to the appropriate Courts for hearing their individual cases. But sometimes the case was one for which the Common Law Courts provided no redress and yet for which some sort of redress ought obviously to be given. So the Chancellor dealt with civil cases of this kind according to his conscience. He was usually a bishop acquainted with Roman and Canon Law, and the principles of these two codes would help him to frame his judgment where the Common Law gave him no guidance. Later Chancellors felt themselves increasingly bound by the decisions of their predecessors, and thus Chancery with its rules of Equity developed into an independent Court of civil law alongside of the Courts of Common Law. The latter were, of course jealous—increasingly so—and would have liked to do away with it. But, though never popular, it was too useful to be spared. And it survived till it was at last amalgamated with the Common Law Courts in 1875.

Thus the Common Law became supreme. It had, by 1875, been virtually supreme for two centuries. But that supremacy was worth little, unless the Courts of Common Law were independent of outside interference. The fact that these Courts had grown up in the shadow of the Crown protected them from interference by anyone else. Nor did the Crown itself interfere with the actual work of the Courts. But it did at times exercise undue influence on judges and juries.

The judges, you see, were at first much too closely bound up with the Executive to escape its influence. To begin with, they were appointed by the King, held office at his good pleasure, and could be dismissed by him. Dismissals were, as a matter of fact, rare in early times, and there appear to have been none in the reign of Elizabeth, but the Stuarts developed a habit of dismissing any judge who questioned the legality of their proceedings, and so, as their proceedings grew more and more doubtfully legal, the number of dismissals increased. James I dismissed at least one, and Charles I three. Charles II got rid of three Lord Chancellors, three Chief Justices and six Judges in twenty-five years, and James II turned out twelve Judges in three years.

But, apart from that, the Judges were the King's recognised counsellors in judicial matters. In the days when the King's Court performed all the functions of government, they had been part of the Executive; they even sat in Parliament; and a trace of their former position still survives, for the Lord Chancellor is a member of the Cabinet and presides over the House of Lords. Later in Tudor times, they were still regularly consulted by the Crown on legal questions, just as the Attorney-General and Solicitor-General are now. Nor was the practice regarded as at all objectionable, until the Stuarts used it to destroy the liberty of the subject. But the Stuarts took to brow-beating the Judges into approving beforehand of matters which would later come before them for decision in the Courts of Law.

Now, since the King appointed the Judges, and

appointed them carefully, most of them were likely anyhow to be champions of the Prerogative. Such was the great Lord Chancellor Bacon. The Judges, he said, should be "lions, but yet lions *under* the throne". The mere fact of holding office would turn others into staunch upholders of authority. It always does. And the rest could usually be intimidated by a royal lecture, backed by the fear of a reprimand in the Star Chamber. But not always. Instance, Sir Edward Coke.

Coke was an obstinate, narrow pedant, consistent only in his blind worship of the Common Law as it stood. In any other age he would have been a nuisance—just as Henry VIII in any other age but *his* would have been a very bad King. But each in his own time and place was just what was wanted. Coke had his first brush with James I in 1607. This is his account of the interview between King and Judges:

"Then the King said that he thought the law was founded upon reason, and that he and others had reason as well as the Judges. To which it was answered by me that true it was God had endowed his Majesty with excellent science and great endowments of nature, but his Majesty was not learned in the laws of his realm of England...; with which the King was greatly offended, and said that he should then be under the law, which was treason to affirm, as he said. To which I said that Bracton saith 'that the King ought not to be under any man, but under God—and the law'."[1]

Such was Coke's influence over his colleagues that, after several further experiences of this nature, the King in 1615 hit on the idea of consulting the Judges singly, instead of, as was the custom, in a body. It was obviously easier for him to bring pressure to bear, if each of them was tackled individually. Coke was horrified at this threat to the independence of the Bench. "Such particular and auricular taking of opinions", he told Bacon, "is not according to the custom of this realm."[2] And, at first, he refused, when his turn came, to give his opinion at all. When at last he did so, it was, needless to say, unfavourable to the King.

The climax was reached in the following year. The King was at Newmarket when a case came before the Courts in which he conceived that his Prerogative was concerned. He sent word to the Judges to postpone their decision until he had spoken with them. They replied, at Coke's instigation, that they were bound by their oaths not to delay justice. On the King's return, they were sent for and lectured by him in the Star Chamber. They all fell on their knees and

[1] Tanner, *English Constitutional Conflicts of the Seventeenth Century*, pp. 36–37.　　　　　　　　　[2] *Ibid.* p. 39.

begged pardon. But Coke, still kneeling, continued to argue. The King then put to each of them the question, whether, in like case again, they *would* stay proceedings. They all said yes, except Coke, who replied ominously that "when that case should be, he would do that should be fit for a judge to do".[1]

That was too much. He was shortly dismissed, and from 1620 till his death in 1634 became the champion of the cause of Common Law in Parliament.

Meanwhile, the practice went on. But at the Restoration there was no longer a Star Chamber with which to overawe the Judges, so Charles II and James II had to make the most of their power of appointment and dismissal. Both packed the Bench with unscrupulous blackguards and subservient toadies who convicted their enemies and legalised their abuse of the Prerogative. It didn't do them any good in the end, for the complaisance of the Judges was one of the chief causes of the Revolution. On William III's accession all ten Judges were summarily dismissed, and soon afterwards in 1701 it was laid down by the Act of Settlement that in future Judges were only to be dismissed on the demand of both Houses of Parliament.

The Judicial Bench had won its independence.

[1] *Ibid.* p. 40.

But its members continued for the most part to be champions of government authority. When, in George III's reign, an unnatural alliance was formed between Royal Prerogative and Parliamentary Privilege against the liberties of the people, it was not the independence of the judges so much as the courage of juries that saved the situation.

They hadn't much courage to start with, poor juries. Sometimes they were packed, and sometimes they were intimidated, fined and imprisoned. The trouble was that they took a long time to live down their origin. That origin is ancient and obscure. It isn't even English. And we needn't poke our noses into it. Enough to say that originally in criminal cases they were the people who accused the prisoner, and in civil cases they were the neighbours who witnessed to the facts of the case. Therefore in early days there was nothing illogical, either in punishing a criminal jury, if the prisoner was acquitted, because the acquittal must mean that the accusation had been false, nor in punishing a civil jury for a perverse verdict, because a perverse verdict must mean that they were false witnesses. But it *was* illogical to go on punishing juries after their character had changed and they had become what they are now, people who find a verdict on the evidence of others.

Nevertheless juries were liable to be called before

the Star Chamber. There were other reasons for this, some good, some bad. Thus, juries were often bribed and often too frightened to bring in even a quite obvious verdict against a powerful person. On the other hand, government used the liability of juries as a means of securing the convictions it wanted.

"If", wrote Sir Thomas Smith in Elizabeth's reign, "If they do pronounce not guilty on the prisoner, against whom manifest witness is brought in, the prisoner escapeth, but the twelve are not only rebuked by the Judges, but also threatened of punishment, and many times commanded to appear in the Star Chamber. But this threatening chanceth oftener than the execution thereof; and the twelve answer with most gentle words, they did it according to their consciences, and pray the judges to be good unto them:...and so it passeth away for the most part. Yet I have seen [them]...in my time not only imprisoned for a space, but a large fine set upon their heads....But these doings were even then accounted of many for violent, tyrannical and contrary to the liberty and custom of the realm of England."[1]

However, the practice still went on, and, after the abolition of the Star Chamber, the Judges took it upon themselves to punish juries for verdicts with which they did not agree. But at last, in a case which

[1] Hallam, *History of England*, vol. I, p. 49 (1897).

occurred in 1670, it was laid down that juries were not liable for verdicts against the evidence or against the direction of the Judge, and that decision finally established their security.

But what about the security of the subject—the ordinary private citizen? How are his rights protected? The Law, it is said, provides a remedy for everyone of his rights, and, if his rights are infringed, he can seek the remedy by appropriate action in the Courts. But suppose he is arrested and put in prison? Then, it is said, he is given a fair trial. But what is there to prevent his being *kept* in prison, without trial, indefinitely?

There was always more than a possibility of this in the bad, old days, and the law even then provided a very simple remedy—the Writ of Habeas Corpus. A prisoner, or any friend of his, could demand as of right from the Court of King's Bench a writ to be addressed to whoever held him in custody, bidding that person "to produce the body of the prisoner with the day and cause of his detention". The prisoner would be brought into Court, the Judge would review the grounds of his commitment, and, according to the circumstances, discharge him, admit him to bail, or remand him in custody pending trial.

You would think that settled it. But it did not. The Privy Council claimed the right to commit persons to prison, and, as a descendant of the old King's Court, it had a perfectly good claim. But the claim was expanded to mean that, on a committal by the Council, a sufficient answer to a Writ of Habeas Corpus was the bare statement that the prisoner had been committed "by special command of the King"—or "Council"—without adding any *cause* for the commitment. The Crown's justification for not showing cause was "reasons of state", and, of course, one can imagine circumstances—such as the unravelling of some widespread conspiracy—when secrecy would be genuinely important. But, obviously, the practice was capable of abuse, and, if no cause was shown on the return to the Writ of Habeas Corpus, the Judges had no means of deciding whether the grounds for commitment were good or bad, and the prisoner had to be left in prison. The Council was thus provided with a very convenient means of keeping anyone in prison indefinitely without trial.

Now this was contrary to Magna Carta and to an Act of 1351. Still, the Judges were in a difficult position, and whenever the matter came before them, they usually hedged. The practice was condemned by the Petition of Right, in 1628, to which Charles gave his consent. But that didn't prevent him from doing much the same thing in the following year, and it wasn't till 1641 that the validity of the Writ of

Habeas Corpus in such cases was finally established by statute.

The Writ was now valid, but it could still be evaded in various ingenious ways—by ignoring it until it had been issued two or three times, by recommitting the prisoner as soon as he had been bailed, by keeping him on the move from one prison to another, or by transferring him to the Channel Islands, where the Writ did not run. The Habeas Corpus Act of 1679 stopped most of these evasions, but that famous guarantee of our freedom only became law by a trick. Here is a contemporary's account of the division in the House of Lords:

"Lord Grey and Lord Norris were named to be the tellers. Lord Norris, being a man subject to vapours, was not at all times attentive to what he was doing; so a very fat Lord coming in, Lord Grey counted him for ten, as a jest at first; but seeing Lord Norris had not observed it, he went on with this misreckoning of ten; so it was reported to the House, and declared that they who were for the Bill were the majority, though it indeed went on the other side; and by this means the Bill passed."[1]

But this Act set no limit to the bail that might be asked, so that it was still possible to keep a man in prison by demanding a greater sum than he could

[1] Burnet, *History of His Own Times*, vol. II, p. 264.

possibly raise. The Bill of Rights in 1689 declared that "excessive Bail ought not to be required", and remaining loopholes were blocked as late as 1816.

In times of national danger or social unrest—for instance during the Jacobite risings and during the French Revolution—the operation of the Writ was sometimes suspended by statute in regard to persons charged with certain specified crimes or treasonable practices. The last occasion in England was in 1817. But in the Great War the same thing was done in a different way. By the Defence of the Realm Acts of 1914, Parliament empowered the Executive to make regulations which had this effect. We all know what happens to liberty in wartime, and many of the regulations issued were wholly illegal. The courage and impartiality shown by the Judges in declaring them so were a welcome reminder that one day freedom might come again. Well, Dora is not dead, and her soul goes marching on.

Now let's take stock. Common Law is supreme; Courts and Judges are independent; Juries are safe; and the citizen is protected by Habeas Corpus. What does all that amount to? It amounts to what is called "The Rule of Law". And, just as it is through the Sovereignty of Parliament that we are able to make new laws to *improve* our freedom, so it is through the

Rule of Law that what freedom we *have* is protected. How then does it protect it?

That very great lawyer, Dicey, summed this up under three heads.[1] Let's take them one by one—only, if you don't mind, I'll take the second one last, because that's the one I want to deal with at length.

"Englishmen are ruled by the Law and the Law alone." That is his first proposition. It means, he says, that no man can be punished except for a breach of the law legally proved in an ordinary Court of Law. Well, that's exactly what I've been explaining in the early part of this talk. So we can pass on—except that I ought perhaps to mention, for purposes of comparison with other nations, that in nearly all continental countries to-day the Executive has wider discretionary powers of arrest and temporary imprisonment than it has here.

Now for Dicey's third proposition. "The Constitution is the result of the ordinary Law of the land." In most foreign countries, where civil liberties still exist, they are secured by the constitution. There is a special law, the constitutional law, and part of it explicitly guarantees the liberty of citizens. Their individual liberties are based on that general guarantee. In England it's exactly the other way round. There is no such general guarantee. There is no such constitu-

[1] Dicey, *The Law of the Constitution.*

tional document. No law or series of laws defines our liberties. The Habeas Corpus Acts, for instance, declare no principles and define no rights. They merely supply a remedy in individual cases. And *all* our liberties are based on particular decisions pronounced by the Courts in individual cases. They are generalisations drawn from individual cases. Thus in 1762 there was no law against slavery in England. But when a negro was brought before the Courts in that year, the Judge laid it down that as soon as a man sets foot on English ground he is free. Similarly, our freedom of speech, freedom of assembly, and so on, depend for their extent and validity on the fact that in past trials of individuals, the Judges have declared this or that to be lawful. To sum it all up in one sentence: In most foreign countries the rights of individuals proceed from principles pronounced in the constitution; in England the so-called principles of the constitution proceed from the rights of individuals as pronounced in individual cases before the Courts.

You may say—that's just a formal distinction. It doesn't prove that liberty is any better our way round than their way round. You're right. It doesn't. In fact, our civil liberties, made up in this way of bits and pieces, are very inadequately defined. We had an instance of that in 1936 in connection with the

Fascist demonstration in the East End of London. But our system—or, if you prefer it, our lack of system—does give us one advantage. Our liberties are harder to take away. Liberties guaranteed in general by one constitutional law are much more easily suspended. There they are all of a piece, all in one place. The government has merely to announce that "the constitutional guarantees are suspended", and bang goes all freedom. And, as a matter of history, they have often been suspended. But you can't do away so easily with an enormous number of particular rights dotted all over the Statute Book and the Law Court Records. Some of the provisions of the Habeas Corpus Act may be suspended, but that's a long way short of a wholesale suspension of constitutional rights. Mind you, we don't deserve any credit. It just happened that way. And it's lucky for us that it did.

And now for Dicey's second proposition: "Equality before the law, or the equal subjection of all classes to the ordinary Law of the land administered by the ordinary Law Courts." Every one of us, from the Prime Minister downwards, be he government official, soldier, policeman, clergyman or private citizen, is responsible for his actions to the ordinary Courts of Law. And, he adds, "individual freedom is thereby more thoroughly protected in England against oppression by the government that in any other European country".

Isn't that lovely? But it's not true. Government officials are no longer amenable for all their actions to the ordinary Courts of Law, and they are developing very extensive legislative and judicial powers of their own. And as this affects you and me and all our liberties very closely, we ought to be clear as to what is happening.

In many foreign countries, France for instance, equality before the law doesn't extend to the government or its servants. Government officials in their official capacities have special rights as against private citizens and are independent of the ordinary Courts of Law. Their rights are defined in a special body of rules called "droit administratif". There is no proper word for it in English. That in itself is significant. But it is usually translated as "administrative law".

In countries where administrative law exists, the Executive has its own courts, its own laws and its own procedure. All cases arising between government officials and private citizens are dealt with in these special courts, and the ordinary courts have no right whatever to interfere.

Now all that is perfectly proper in its proper place. But, as Lord Chief Justice Hewart says, "it is a system which is fundamentally opposed to the English conception of 'the Rule of Law'".[1] Dicey before he died noticed that something like it was beginning to crop up in England. The crop has spread and ripened since then.

You know what a lot of social legislation comes before Parliament every year. It's tremendously complicated, and Parliament hasn't time to work out every detail. So Parliament tends to lay down the general principles only and to authorise the Minister of the appropriate government department to fill in the details as he sees fit after the Bill has become law. Now that in itself means handing over extensive law-making power to government departments. Still, if those powers are properly limited by the statute, the Law Courts can always be appealed to, if the Minister exceeds those powers. For instance, in 1920, a man tried to recover possession of his house. He found that not only he couldn't get it back, but that he had exposed himself to fine and imprisonment for having tried to do so. For the government, under powers conferred by D.O.R.A., had commandeered his and other houses, and further made a rule that anyone who tried to recover possession would be guilty of a summary offence. However, when the man very naturally appealed, the Courts

[1] Hewart, *The New Despotism*, p. 37.

held that the government in making that rule had exceeded its powers.

But in some cases the Courts are rendered powerless to give redress. By the Small Holdings Act, 1908, County Councils might make orders, subject to their confirmation by the Board of Agriculture, for the compulsory purchase of land. But the Act stated that these authorities were to "avoid taking an undue or inconvenient quantity of land from any one owner or tenant". Mr Ringer, a Norfolk farmer, accordingly appealed to the Courts against the compulsory purchase of one of his farms, because without it he couldn't profitably work his other farms. The Courts, however, were unable to help him, because another section of the Act declared that the confirmation by the Board of Agriculture of an order was in itself to be taken as proof that that order was legal. In short, the Board could exceed its powers as much as it liked with impunity.

In other cases, you can't appeal to a Court at all. The Act definitely says you mayn't. Take the Roads Act, 1920. The decision of the Minister is—to quote the Act itself—"final and not subject to appeal in any Court". But what was described at the time as "the high-water mark" was reached by the Rating and Valuation Act, 1925. Section 67 authorises the Minister *to do anything* he likes for the purpose of

bringing certain provisions of the Act into operation. And it is expressly stated that he may even
modify the provisions of the Act itself. It seems
hardly worth while Parliament bothering to frame
an Act at all, if the Minister can alter it as he
likes.

Have you any idea of the amount and extent of
these Regulations? I haven't. They increase so rapidly
that only Einstein could keep track of them. But in
1927 alone, 1349 *sets* of rules were officially registered
(and mind you they don't all have to be registered)
and twenty-six more Acts of Parliament enabling
such rules to be made were added to the Statute
Book. And they deal with every subject under the
sun, from Electricity to Education, including National
Health Insurance, Old Age Pensions, Town Planning
and Trade Marks.

Still, there they are—most of them, anyway—and,
if we want to, we can look them up, though we
shouldn't understand them, if we did. But how are
they applied? That's not easy to find out, because
they are applied, not publicly, but in private. Anyway
the Minister (and that, of course, means his government department) makes the rules and also applies
them. However impartial he may be, he is acting
as judge in his own cause.

Those with most experience of the procedure are

anything but satisfied with it. Let me quote the late Balfour Browne, K.C., as an example:

"An Inspector is sent down and pretends to listen to the evidence and the arguments of counsel and makes his report, and then a very clever department, that does not know the place or its surroundings, that has heard nothing of the case, sets aside the decision of its own Inspector upon grounds which are not made public. It makes the local inquiry a farce."

Lord Hewart confirms that it is not usual for the department to give any reason for its decision. But in some cases an appeal is possible to Referees. The Minister then does state his reasons. But, to quote another authority, the Minister's statement is couched in such obscure and formal language that "the appellant is absolutely bewildered and has not the slightest idea how to reply".

You see how these ministerial powers violate the principle of the Rule of Law. But I would like you also to notice their effect on the supremacy of Parliament. Because, as I said, the Sovereignty of Parliament and the Rule of Law are the two foundations of our freedom.

Parliament may remain technically sovereign, but in practice it surrenders a lot of its law-making power to the ministry. All these Regulations are made by ministers in their government departments. Most of them don't have to be submitted to Parliament at all. If they are submitted, it is often in a perfunctory way. A glaring instance occurred in December 1934. The Unemployment Act of that year set up a Board to draft Regulations for Unemployment Assistance. These Regulations were to be submitted for acceptance or rejection to Parliament. But Parliament was only able to accept or reject them as a whole. It couldn't amend them. This really was rather odd. Parliament, we are told, can do *anything* except make a man a woman. Yet here we see Parliament unable to amend Regulations drawn up on Parliament's own instructions by a body which Parliament had itself created.

But the real danger to Parliament is this: the habit of passing laws in skeleton form may be extended indefinitely. The main safeguard of our political liberty is that all measures are publicly debated in Parliament before they become law. They are reported and commented on in the Press. The public is aware of them, and its opinion makes itself felt. But suppose a government came into power that was impatient of such procedure and wanted to short-circuit both Parliament and public opinion. It might adopt the proposal of the Socialist League and pass an omnibus Emergency Powers Act, conferring unlimited power on the ministry. The government could then behind our backs make any laws it liked in the form of Regulations and dragoon us into obedience.

So, although it may seem silly to insist on strict adherence to the principle of the Rule of Law, we must remember that that principle is not just a bit of nonsense suddenly invented. It took centuries to develop, and it wouldn't have developed all that time unless it really was valuable and suited our needs. And once you start messing about with a principle like that—even though your intentions are quite harmless, and the thing you want to do is in itself quite a good thing—once you start messing about with it even mildly, you may soon find you've done irreparable damage.

But we must be fair. What defence has been put forward to justify all these legislative and judicial powers of government departments? Firstly, it is said, you can't have all this social legislation without a lot of Regulations. Well, we'll all grant that. Secondly, Parliament hasn't time to frame them all in detail. About that I'd like to observe, that if the Legislature hasn't time to get through all the necessary legislation, then there must be something wrong with the Legislature. And it seems more sensible to reform the Legislature so that it can do its own job properly, than to hand over legislation to the Executive, which isn't a Legislature at all. But let that pass. The argument goes on: Parliament doesn't know the ins and outs of administrative work and is therefore incompetent to frame Regulations for the Administration to use. Look how badly worded some statutes are. But that argument really won't wash. The Regulations made by government departments are notorious for their clumsiness.

I have before me two letters recently published in *The Times*. One is from an eminent lawyer, Sir Benjamin Cohen, who is himself a Referee administering Regulations under the Widows' and Old Age Pensions Acts. The Regulations, he says, "are so framed that a trained lawyer cannot interpret them with any degree of certainty....A great injustice is done to the poor applicant." The other letter is from The Secretary to the National Federation of Insurance Workers. "On behalf of some 25,000 insurance agents engaged in the work of approved societies", he writes to say that "the truth of the matter is that the agents, like all engaged in this work, are utterly bewildered by the complications and technicalities of the innumerable regulations."

When it comes to defending the judicial powers of government departments, the argument put forward is that the Law Courts are too slow and too expensive. Decisions must be made cheaply and promptly, therefore the ministry must make them. Well, it's perfectly true that legal procedure *is* cumbersome, expensive and slow. I shall have more to say about that later on. But is administrative procedure any better? We've already seen that it isn't simple. Is it cheaper? Cheaper to the *applicant* it may be— though, to quote an old saying: "Costly justice is better than cheap injustice." But is it cheaper to the community? Sir Benjamin Cohen says that in 1925 there were two Referees to administer the Act. There are now fifteen. "This involves", he continues, "a corresponding increase in the number of Registrars and also a large increase in the number of inspectors all over the country.... This will give some indication of the expense involved." And as for speediness of decision, another authority writes: "Nine months is quite a usual time to wait, and I should say about the average period taken for the Minister to come to a decision.... Other cases have taken over a year, and I have known of cases which have taken two years to settle."

Not long ago I had a talk myself with a Civil Servant. After going over the familiar arguments, he said: "You see, it's like this. A Pensions' scheme or an Insurance scheme is a very elaborate and technical business. We do know more about it than Parliament does, and we frame the best scheme possible. Now if Parliament tinkers with it, or the Courts of Law pick holes in it, the whole scheme may be ruined."—"Yes," I said, "but don't you see that's the old argument of the Tudors and Stuarts. It's the argument of all totalitarian states—Fascist or Communist—to-day. It's always been the defence put forward for interfering with other people's liberty. 'We can give you better government than you could give yourselves.' In short, 'Mother knows best', they say. But a free man prefers to be his own judge of what is good government. And you can't be free, unless the making of the laws that govern you and their application in individual cases are publicly ventilated. And that ventilation, even if it's a bit draughty, is better than the best bureaucratic phug in the world." Strange to relate, he said he agreed with me.

To sum up the defence then, it is fair to say that those who approve of a certain amount of administrative law as inevitable and even desirable, consider that—to quote one of them—"bureaucratic justice as at present administered is not in the true interests of the public. Rights that are most vital to the public are nowadays disposed of with varying degrees of secrecy in Government offices".

Well, what's to be done about it? That's up to you. I've stated the problem, and I hope you'll discuss it among yourselves. But let me in conclusion drop this pebble into the pool.

I think a special committee should be appointed at once to overhaul and simplify the indigestible mass of existing Regulations. That would at least clear up the present mess. But it wouldn't, of course, solve the problem. To that solution, three things, I think, are necessary. First, powers granted to a Minister in any Act should be definitely and clearly limited in that Act. Secondly, Parliament should retain effective powers of accepting, amending, or rejecting Regulations when made, and should periodically review their working. There might be a permanent committee for this purpose.

And lastly, Common Law procedure should be made much simpler, cheaper and quicker; administrative tribunals, in so far as they are unavoidable, should be definite bodies, properly appointed and publicly known; and there should in the last resort be a power of appeal from ministerial decisions to an independent Court of Record sitting in public.

Anyway, something ought to be done about it, I think—and soon. Don't you?

VI

FREEDOM AND PARLIAMENT

LET'S forget for the moment all we know about Parliament to-day. We are back in the thirteenth century. Imagine a large oblong room. At one end is the King on his throne. In the centre are four large woolsacks on which officials and judges sit facing one another. Down each side wall are long parallel benches on which sit the King's most important tenants—bishops and abbots and priors to right of him, earls and barons to left of him. That is a Parliament in the Parliament Chamber.

But where are the Commons? They aren't there. This is a meeting of the King's Court. They don't belong. But it isn't true that there aren't any common people about, because anyone can bring a petition to the King's Court. And the King himself sometimes sends for local representatives to come and tell him what is happening in their part of the country.

How, then, did the Commons become a part of Parliament? Well, it was like this. The King needed money to carry on the government. He was supposed to manage with the income from his own lands and the rents of his tenants. But he wasn't just a landlord. He was the King of England. Surely the whole nation ought to contribute to the national exchequer. And it was soon found that the most convenient way of getting it to do so was to summon, whenever money was wanted, representatives of every county and of the wealthiest towns to attend a meeting of Parliament. That established a first principle. "No Taxation without Representation."

Now see what happens. Parliament is sitting. Money is wanted. The representatives have been summoned. They arrive. Parliament suspends its ordinary business. The representatives are ushered in. They stand sheepishly at the far end of the Chamber opposite the throne. There is the King, and there are all the greatest men in England. Very alarming. The Chancellor speaks. He tells them what the King needs. Silence. He says they had better go and agree upon their answer. Out they go. I don't suppose they take long about it at first. For one thing people from different parts of the country would hardly understand each other's language. When they've made up their minds, they troop back again. But they can't all speak at once. They have to have a mouthpiece. Hence the Speaker. And to this day, at the beginning and end of Parliaments, the Speaker appears with the Commons at the Bar of what is now the House of Lords. But in those days, having given their answer, they are sent home, and Parliament resumes its interrupted work. You see, they aren't yet a part of Parliament, these representatives, nor are they summoned to all Parliaments. They are just a temporary excrescence on an occasional Parliament.

But not for long. They begin to bargain with the King. They bring petitions with them like everybody else. If the King wants their money, he must grant their petitions. What is more, he must promise to grant them before they go home. And to prevent any hocus-pocus behind their backs, they start drawing up the Bills themselves, as they do to-day, and they don't grant their money till the Bills have been passed into law.

Here's a second principle established. "Taxation is granted in return for redress of grievances." But redressing grievances takes time—the *whole* of Parliament's time. So the Commons had to be there throughout the whole session. In fact, they soon had to be summoned to every session. But travelling wasn't easy in those days. To get all the representatives together was an elaborate business. Besides, the King didn't want to be criticised, and the Commons didn't want to be taxed. So Parliaments became less frequent. The gaps grew wider and wider, till it looked as though Parliament might disappear altogether—as did similar assemblies abroad.

It was the Tudors who restored and built up the power of Parliament. They needed its support—and especially the support of the Commons. So they installed the Commons in St Stephen's chapel, which was part of the Palace of Westminster. It became the *House* of Commons. Thus the Parliament Chamber ceased to be any longer the whole of Parliament; it became merely the *House* of Lords. And the House of Lords came to regard itself as the proper place for peers and bishops only. Anyone else was only present on sufferance. So the officials, who sat on those four central woolsacks and weren't peers, left the House of Lords where they were looked down upon and joined up with the Commons, where they were very much looked up to. And that's how ministers came to sit in the House of Commons. Only the Chancellor remained in the House of Lords, whether he was a peer or not. He had to, because then, as now, he presided over the House. But, later on, if he wasn't a peer, he was invariably made one, so that he might match his surroundings.

Parliament, then, had taken on its modern shape. And now that the Church had been nationalised and the feudal powers of the barons destroyed, it was without a rival. It was already the Sovereign Parliament it is to-day. But the two Houses, of course, have since then undergone many changes, both in character and in strength. Of the House of Lords I need only say, that as more and more peers were created, its numbers doubled and redoubled and doubled again. As its numbers increased, so its importance declined. For a long time it held its own with the Commons, partly because of the wealth and prestige of its members, and partly because of their enormous influence in the constituencies. But with the growth of democracy in the nineteenth century, it sank to a definitely subordinate position. Its legal powers, however, remained unimpaired till 1911. By the Parliament Act of that year it has lost all power over Money Bills and can hold up the passage of other Bills only temporarily.

The Commons in Tudor times were still very much on the make. Henry VIII encouraged them: "We be informed by our judges", he told them once in an expansive mood, "that we at no time stand so highly in our estate royal, as in the time of Parliament, wherein we as head, and you as members, are conjoined and knit together in one body politic."[1]

But if he could flatter, he could also snub. This is how he is said to have treated them when they opposed his Bill for the Dissolution of the Monasteries: "When

[1] Pollard, *The Evolution of Parliament*, p. 231.

the Bill was stuck long in the Lower House and could get no passage he commanded the Commons to attend him in the forenoon in his gallery, where he let them wait till late in the afternoon; and then coming out of his Chamber, walking a turn or two amongst them and looking angrily on them, first on the one side, then on the other, at last; 'I hear', (saith he) 'that my bill will not pass; but I will have it pass, or I will have some of your heads'."[1]

Elizabeth liked Parliament less than did her father. She told the Commons that, "they should do well to meddle with no matters of state but such as should be propounded unto them."[2] But, in practice, at one time or another, every matter of state was propounded to them, so that by the end of the century they had precedents and experience enough to have a policy and leaders of their own.

And when James tried to adopt the same attitude, they told him that it was "an ancient, general and undoubted right of Parliament to debate freely all matters which do properly concern the subject".[3] In 1621, he returned to the charge, and this time the Commons pulled out all the stops of the organ in their reply:

[1] Spelman, *History of Sacrilege*, 1632 (ed. 1853), p. 206.
[2] Prothero, *Statutes and Constitutional Documents*, p. 119.
[3] *Ibid.* p. 297.

"The liberties, franchises, privileges, and jurisdictions of parliament are the ancient and undoubted
birthright and inheritance of the subjects of England;
and the arduous and urgent affairs concerning the
king, state, and defence of the realm, and of the
church of England, and the maintenance and making
of laws, and redress of mischiefs and grievances, which
daily happen within this realm, are proper subjects
and matters of counsel and debate in parliament."[1]

James tore that page out of the Journals of the
House. But that was a sign of weakness. He was
losing control. A few years later, when Charles I
ordered the Commons to adjourn, they held the
Speaker down in his chair; and while the King was
sending for his guards, and his messengers were
banging on the door, resolutions were put and carried,
declaring anyone who advised the doing of certain
things, which in fact the King was doing, to be "a
betrayer of the liberties of England and an enemy
of the same".[2]

The King's last hold on the House was the Speaker,
for the Speaker was a royal nominee. But even the
Speaker failed Charles I. On that famous occasion
in 1642, when Charles broke into the House, with

[1] Prothero, *op. cit.* pp. 313–314.
[2] Gardiner, *Constitutional Documents of the Puritan Revolution*,
pp. 82–83.

114

four hundred armed men at his back, to arrest five members for treason, he asked the Speaker if he saw them in the House. "May it please your Majesty," replied the Speaker on his knees, "I have neither eyes to see, nor tongue to speak in this place, but as this House is pleased to direct me, whose servant I am here."[1] The Speaker was no longer the agent of the Crown, but the servant of the House itself.

In short, the Commons were now strong enough to defy the Crown. And it took, first a rebellion in which one King lost his head, and then a revolution by which another lost his throne, to decide the issue between them.

With the revolution political sovereignty passed to Parliament. But not to the people. For Parliament meant the gentry both at Westminster and in the constituencies. Political liberty had become the privilege of a few hundred families. Not that they thought about it like that. Liberty had been won. The constitution was safe. There was nothing more to be done. So they sat back contented, grew rich, built up those great estates that are now being broken up again, and once a year solemnly celebrated "the Glorious Revolution". They were still celebrating it when the French Revolution broke out exactly a

[1] Tanner, *English Constitutional Conflicts of the Seventeenth Century*, p. 114.

century later and startled them out of their complacency.

But if Parliament was out of touch with the people, it was not so much their fault as the result of an antiquated distribution of the franchise, which everyone took for granted. It had been fixed long ago by statute, or charter, or custom, and by the eighteenth century had become arbitrary, narrow, haphazard and absurd. And though it was by no means confined to one class, in practice the constituencies had passed into the control of great men and local gentry. In fact, the franchise had become a form of property which could be bought or inherited. Why should a member feel responsible to his constituency? Most of the inhabitants had no voice in his election, and those who had were paid.

But once in Parliament he could hope to recoup his election expenses, provided he voted for the government. For the Crown had enormous patronage. It had jobs and pensions to give away, government contracts to place, loans to issue at high rates of interest, even lottery tickets to distribute. Parliament was the path to promotion in every walk of life, even in the army and navy. No one was in politics for his health.

This state of things might have gone on indefinitely, if George III hadn't made a last bid to restore the royal power. His method was simple. He took the royal patronage out of the hands of his Whig ministers and used it to build up a party of his own. With a majority of his own in Parliament, he could use parliamentary privilege to support royal prerogative, and these two together could defy the nation. They did. And it was in opposition to this unnatural alliance that the British people at last learnt the true meaning of political liberty. The American colonies found it in rebellion and independence; in England it started the movement for Reform.

The two very different men who in very different ways started the ball rolling were Burke and Wilkes. Edmund Burke was an Irishman of humble birth who by sheer genius worked his way up to a leading position among the aristocratic Whigs. He didn't believe in franchise reform. He idealised the constitution as it was. And he couldn't abide vague, abstract generalisations about "the Rights of Man", which were fashionable among Reformers. In their concern for man's rights, he thought, these quacks forgot his nature; and one can't help feeling he would have been a good man to have about the place to-day, when civilisation is being offered so many infallible patent medicines. But though he abhorred revolution, he did believe in evolution, and that was much more important in his day than it may sound to us, because it undermined that static view of society which made eighteenth-century politicians regard the Glorious Revolution as final and perfect. And, as a practical contribution to reform, he secured the passage of Bills which did at least reduce corruption both in Parliament and the constituencies.

John Wilkes wasn't a gentleman either, but he was such good company that he passed for one. He was one of those irrepressible bounders who can get away with murder. Not that he ever committed one. But his private life was scandalous. When offered snuff, he said: "No, thank you. I have no *small* vices." And his public life was a series of escapades that were partly ludicrous and partly heroic. His popularity was immense—especially among the poor. When told that one of his supporters had turned his coat, he replied: "Impossible. Not one of them has a coat to turn." Eighteenth-century politicians knew something of the fury of the mob, but they had no idea of the force of public opinion till Wilkes showed them. With scarcely any backing, except that of public opinion, he carried on a continuous guerilla warfare against royal prerogative, government tyranny and parliamentary privilege. Into all that I haven't time to go. But Wilkes is important, not for what he did, but for the issues he raised, and at one time or another he raised practically every issue of importance concerning freedom and the constitution. He advocated radical parliamentary reform. And in his mouth political liberty meant, not the privileges of some, but the rights of all. Scamp he may have been, but he deserved his epitaph: "A Friend of Liberty."

The Reform movement had started. Societies were founded, petitions presented, resolutions passed, bills introduced. The Americans talked it. The French talked it. Ah, but that was just the trouble. First the American war, then the French Revolution, and then the wars with France made all such agitation seem unpatriotic, seditious. Respectable people pursed their lips; societies closed down or were suppressed. Except for a few unpopular enthusiasts, the movement was dead.

But when it revived after the war, it was a genuinely popular movement, whereas before it had been rather highbrow and academic. For a time that made matters worse. Any agitation among the poor made the middle classes nervous. But it soon became clear, that the choice lay between radical reform by revolution and moderate reform by Parliament. And once that was realised opposition petered out.

The Reform Act of 1832 enfranchised the middle classes. Many regarded it as final. But that it could not be. The pass had been sold. The old franchise had been regarded as sacrosanct. It was the ancient right and untouchable privilege of certain places and people. But change it once and you could change it again. So the Reform Act of 1867 enfranchised the town artisan; the Act of 1884 the agricultural labourer; and the Acts of 1918 and 1928 put women on the same terms as men.

Parliament and adult suffrage. Therein lies our political freedom. What does it amount to?

Parliament consists of King, Lords and Commons. But of these three, only the last is elected by the people. Are the other two, then, obstacles to our political freedom?

The Crown's relations to Parliament are to-day normally so purely formal that they need no discussion. But when a crisis arises, or when the correct constitutional procedure is in doubt, the King's authority is very real and very necessary. Recent instances are: the deadlock over the Parliament Bill, 1910–11, and the rival claims in 1923 of Lord Curzon and Mr Baldwin to be Prime Minister. The position of the Crown on these occasions is not a very enviable one. But the King, being above party, is more likely to be impartial in his interpretation of public opinion than any politician. And in the last resort his decision is subject to the verdict of the people at the polls. So I don't think the power of the Crown can be regarded as infringing our political freedom.

But the House of Lords, some people think, does infringe it. And they have a strong case. The House of Lords started as an assembly of royal officials, eminent ecclesiastics, and the King's most important tenants. These tenants, because their lands were hereditary, made their dignity hereditary, even if they got rid of their lands. They turned their *obligation* to attend Parliament, if the King wanted them to, into a *right* to attend, if they themselves wanted to. New peerages were granted as political patronage and sought after for social advantage, till their number has increased tenfold. The ecclesiastics, who were at first in the majority, have sunk to an insignificant minority. Originally representative of the only Church in the country, they now represent only one Church out of many. As for the royal officials, they have been eliminated altogether, except those of them who happen to be peers. New elements have been introduced, such as representative peers of Scotland elected for each Parliament, representative peers of Ireland elected for life, and the Law Lords whose peerage is not hereditary at all. As a result, the House is now based on no recognisable plan or principle, but is an unwieldy, illogical, undemocratic body, five-sixths of whose work is done by one-sixth of its members.

Oh, yes. It's easy to poke fun at the House of

Lords. Everybody does it. But I rather wonder if it isn't a crowning illustration of our national inability to create new institutions, and our genius for making even the oldest and most illogical of them work.

The House of Lords may be illogical, but it does work. And that's something. Whether it works well or badly depends on what we consider to be its job. What *is* the proper function of a second chamber in this country? Do we need one at all? And if so what do we want it for? The conventional answer is that we need a second chamber to check the first.—A bit odd that!—You believe in democracy, and you want to check it. A better view surely is to regard a second chamber as a democracy's second thoughts. The House of Commons is overworked. A second chamber can correct slipshod and doubtful phrasing in hastily passed Bills. It can debate matters which the Commons have no time to debate properly—imperial and foreign affairs especially—and it can discuss subjects which the Commons do not deal with at all because they are not in the forefront of party politics.

But surely what is required for these purposes is not so much a second legislative body composed of party politicians, as a sort of council composed of people distinguished in every sphere of life, with sufficient leisure and detachment from daily political strife to be calm in their deliberations and independent in their judgments. It isn't easy to get such a body together by democratic means. And, when all is said and done, the effective membership of the House of Lords, by which I mean those members who actually attend and function, *is* something like a body of this sort and *does* do this sort of work.

Ah, you say, but something else could do it better —better anyway than an exclusive club of hereditary peers. Now heredity is not to be sneezed at. Ask the scientists. Look up the family trees of some of our' statesmen. What about the Cecils, for instance? And another thing: Heredity breeds tradition, and there's a lot to be said for tradition, especially in this country where the law is based on custom.

What are the alternatives to Heredity? Nomination and Election. But nomination by a King or other independent Head of a state is as undemocratic as an hereditary peerage, and nomination by an elected government is only a form of indirect election. And in a democracy an elected second chamber will only be respected, will only be strong, in so far as it represents public opinion as closely as the first. You can get a difference between the chambers by insisting that candidates for the second chamber shall be of a certain age or standing, that they shall be elected for a longer period, be indirectly elected—and so on. There are lots of devices. The trouble is that in this way you tend to get a second chamber that isn't democracy's second thoughts but its thoughts of years ago. Or you can get a difference by adopting some form of Proportional Representation in electing your second chamber. It will then represent the people even more closely than the first. It may, in fact, be a dangerous rival to it. In short, a weak elected second chamber will command no respect, a strong one may command too much.

I leave the solution of this problem to you with a reminder that as a race we are bad innovators, but good adaptors—and with a warning, if you think the House of Lords funny, to be careful you don't get something less amusing and much more objectionable.

Now for the House of Commons. It is the vehicle of our political freedom. The question, therefore, arises: "Is it *truly* representative?" The old criterion was: One man, one vote; one vote, one value. Well, we've gone farther than "one man, one vote"—since women have the vote as well as men—but not so far as "one vote, one value". Under our system of voting it's not possible. A candidate is elected whether his majority is one or ten thousand, and the votes given against him go for nothing. To give a single illustration: At the 1906 election in Wales the Liberals polled just twice as many votes as the Conservatives, but they didn't get merely twice as many Welsh seats in Parliament, they got the whole lot, thirty-four, and the Conservatives got none. We could get nearer to "one vote, one value" if we adopted Proportional Representation. And theoretically, I suppose, we should. It is fairer. It is more democratic. But in practice it may have unfortunate results.

It gives fairer representation to minorities, but though that may be necessary when minorities are persecuted, it does not otherwise work satisfactorily. For one thing, it encourages enthusiasts for a particular cause—smoke abatement, say, or birth control—to put a single issue before general issues. For another, it multiplies candidates at the poll, and that means more parties in the House, which leads to undesirable bargaining between groups for mutual support. Lastly, it tends to undermine strong government. By our simple system of voting, the majority in the House gets, if you like, a bigger majority than it deserves. But experience shows everywhere that nothing is more disastrous in a democracy than governments with majorities so small or unreliable that they cannot govern properly.

There is a more fundamental criticism of our political liberty. Government by the people, it is said, is merely a rhetorical phrase. All it amounts to, is this. Once in every five years we are allowed to vote for one of two political programmes put forward by candidates whom we do not know and have probably never seen. Well, I don't know what more we can expect. Frequent elections are a curse. Nearly all modern political questions are too technical for any but experts. We are only equal to giving occasionally a general amateur verdict. We are bad legislators, because we have neither the knowledge nor the time to master the subjects, but we are not bad *judges* of legislation, because we experience its results. And, as we have noticed in earlier talks, the government does, as a matter of fact, show increasing sensitiveness to public opinion.

Still, we have to face the fact that universal suffrage has not done what was expected of it. The enthusiasts of the nineteenth century saw in it the cure for all evils. It would usher in the millennium. It hasn't. Economic liberty, social liberty—these and many others have lagged behind. What is life without a living? What is freedom without the means to use it? Must we then despair?—No. The mistake was to regard political liberty as the *whole* of liberty. It isn't that. It is only an essential part of it. But it has given us control over Parliament, and Parliament is sovereign. There is no fixed and rigid constitution, as in some countries, to block our progress. There is no supreme court to declare our statutes illegal.

Sovereignty is not divided. Parliament is supreme. And through it we can remedy what is wrong and make good what is lacking. For, if political liberty is not the whole of freedom, it is in this country the gateway to it. And the gateway is now open.

VII

FREEDOM AND TRADE

IN previous talks I tried to show how we got our religious liberty, civil liberty and political liberty. But social liberty, we found, had somehow got left behind. Why? Well, that's what I want to inquire into now. The explanation must lie somewhere in the history of our economic organisation.

Nowadays eighty per cent. of our population lives in towns, but until late in the eighteenth century England was mainly an agricultural country.

In early times, life in the country was based on the manor. Imagine a village clustering round a crossroads, church and manor standing back; and round the village three enormous open fields cultivated in rotation, two at a time. About half the land belongs to the lord of the manor, the rest to his tenants. But nobody's land lies all in one piece. The fields are divided into long narrow strips, and each person's holding is made up of a number of these strips scattered all over the fields. Beyond the fields are pasture, woodland and waste. Over these everybody has a right to graze a fixed number of beasts and to cut a fixed amount of fuel and timber.

Land is paid for, not with rent, but with service. The lord of the manor owes certain services to his superior lord. His tenants have to cultivate his land for him—two or three days a week, perhaps, and a bit more at harvest-time. They are, in fact, serfs. But they get a measure of protection in the custom of the manor, by which the lord usually considers himself bound, although it cannot be legally enforced against him.

Now look at the town. Life in the towns is based on the gild. Every craft, that is, every industry, has its craft-gild. Those who follow the same trade live close together in the same quarter of the town. They all belong to their craft-gild. They *must*, because it has a monopoly of that craft in that town. And the gild acts as a religious, charitable, social and economic organisation for the benefit and discipline of its members. It insists on a certain standard of material and workmanship; it fixes conditions of employment; it looks after sick members, and so on. Within the gild are three grades of workers: the apprentice who is learning the trade; the journeyman who earns wages, and the master—which is what every journeyman hopes one day to become. The master sets up shop on his own account. He may, if he likes, employ journeymen and train apprentices. He buys his own materials, works them up on his own premises, and sells them to the public as they pass in the street. He is manufacturer and shopkeeper in one.

There are one or two things we should take note of in this mediaeval economy. In the first place, it isn't the *state's* job. Agriculture is regulated by the custom of the manor, industry by the gild. Secondly, production is on a small scale. Skill and reputation are more important than capital. Wages, production and profit are regulated in the interests of producer and consumer alike, according to the universally held principle of a "just price". And a just price means a proper remuneration for workers, a sound standard of workmanship, and a reasonable profit on sales. I don't say that always happened, but that was the idea. Social security was put before individual enterprise.

It's a very neat pattern, that society. But not very adaptable. Everybody has his place and must stick there. It's rather like one of those boxes of mixed biscuits, in which every variety from the most gaudy and sugary down to the humblest and plainest has its own compartment. But look. Take some biscuits out of one compartment, put more than the right number into another, and give the box a kick. The whole thing becomes a shambles. And that's just what happened to mediaeval society.

First came the Black Death, that appalling plague that wiped out half the population. Then the development of the cloth trade. Hitherto wool had been our mainstay, but refugees taught us to make decent cloth, and in those days, remember, cloth was the only wear, if you couldn't afford silks and furs. So trade ceased to be parochial. It became national and, as foreign trade developed, international. That needed capital. Then the New World was discovered and its riches. Gold and silver poured into Europe. Prices rose all round. On top of the new discoveries came the Reformation. Together they widened the intellectual horizon. They undermined tradition. The Reformation was an expression of spiritual individualism, and the discoveries stimulated individual enterprise. Capital and Individualism, that's what it all boiled down to.

Now see the effect on town and country.

In the country after the Black Death there remained the same work to be done and only half the number of people to do it. Labour was scarce. Labour made demands. It was no good the lord insisting on his customary rights. The serf knew that, if he ran away, anyone would take him on, and take him on at a wage. Serfdom was doomed. And the lord of the manor, unable to get his lands cultivated himself, took to letting them out for a term of years to others, and that gave rise to a farmer class.

But a century later the lord had his revenge. The cloth trade meant an enormously increased demand for wool. Sheep-raising became more profitable than agriculture. It also needed much less labour. But the open field system with its scattered strips was a nuisance. So the landlords did away with it. They turned the peasants off their holdings, enclosed the fields and converted them to pasture.

All these changes had two far-reaching results. First, farming was no longer carried on for sub-sistence, but for profit. It, too, had become a capitalistic enterprise. And, secondly, the serf was replaced by the agricultural labourer. And that explains what is, perhaps, the most distinctive feature of the English land system. In most countries abroad, the serf became in time a peasant proprietor. In England instead of peasant proprietors we have agricultural labourers.

In the towns, too, mediaeval economy was upset. The cloth industry outgrew the capacity of the woollen gilds. The wool had to be grown, to be bought, to be carded and spun. The yarn had to be woven into cloth. The cloth had to be felted and cleansed. The consumer was no longer at the producer's door. He might be hundreds of miles away. He might be abroad. A middleman was necessary, a capitalist who would see the business through from start to finish, from raw material to market. And that's what the clothier henceforth did.

Now all this dislocation of markets and labour inevitably resulted in unemployment and unrest. Beggars wandered over the country in dangerous gangs.

> When Adam delved and Eve span,
> Who was *then* the gentleman?

asked the beggars. And

> Hark, hark!
> The dogs do bark;
> The beggars are coming to town!

answered the terrified townsfolk as they bolted their doors.

Well, of course, the state *had* to step in. Ever since the Black Death government had been tinkering in a bewildered sort of way. And the experiments of two centuries were codified in two great Acts passed, one at the beginning, the other at the end, of Elizabeth's reign.

Entrance to all trades is to be by seven years' apprenticeship. That qualifies a man to earn a wage. Wages are to be fixed annually by Justices of the Peace. Work is compulsory for the able-bodied. If a man *can't* find work, the parish must provide material for him to work on. If he *won't* work, he is to be severely punished. And for the impotent and sick, relief is to be provided by a compulsory poor-rate levied on the parish.

Notice that labour and poverty have become the concern of the state. It hadn't been so before, and it ceased to be so later. But it was a precedent. And as a first attempt to tackle these most difficult of problems I think it's really rather marvellous—in its honesty, its thoroughness and its discrimination. We were the only country to possess such a code permanently. It lasted till the eighteenth century— till the complications brought about by the Industrial Revolution and the ruthlessness of *laissez-faire* rendered it unworkable. It wasn't till the nineteenth century that social conscience began to stir again. And even now we have hardly got as far in solving *our* labour problem, as the Elizabethans got in solving theirs.

We can pass over the next century and a half. Capital and individual enterprise went on expanding, but developments were not so fast or far-reaching as to alter materially the structure of society. Then in the eighteenth century came two economic revolutions, one agricultural, the other industrial.

In the country, a tremendous advance in agricultural science made possible larger and richer crops and bigger and better herds and flocks. But the new technique required more capital and was more economical if applied on a larger scale. So more land was enclosed; farms grew bigger, and the small land-owner was bought out. This, too, was the period when the aristocracy built up their great family estates, and when men who had made money in finance or trade also bought land, because to become a land-owner was to become a gentleman. All these changes brought about a widening of the social gulfs between landlord, farmer and labourer, but also much better farming and the production of much more food. And this last was very essential. England still relied almost entirely for food on what she could produce herself, and the population increased by fifty per cent. in the last half of the eighteenth century and doubled itself again in the first half of the nineteenth.

Thus there grew up the land system which has only recently begun to disappear—the squire who owns the village and all the land of the parish, and on whom are dependent all the farmers, tradesmen and labourers of the district. We may criticise that system nowadays from the social point of view, but it certainly was efficient. As late as the second half of the nine-teenth century it was still being held up to admiration by foreign authorities as a model to be envied and, if possible, copied.

The Industrial Revolution had, socially speaking, much more serious consequences. It was due, of course, to the invention of machinery. Machinery driven by power could only be worked in a factory. And the factory with its aggregation of a number of workers attending on power machinery and directed by a capitalist employer who is both owner and manager—that is the essential characteristic of the Industrial Revolution.

Well, it brought about a tremendous enlargement and cheapening of production and a tremendous extension of trade. That led to a tremendous improvement in transport, a tremendous increase in population and a tremendous expansion of national wealth. No harm in all that.

But the attendant social upheaval was disastrous. The old mediaeval ideals, which still survived in a modified form, were completely destroyed. The idea of a just price for labour and product gave way to the iron law of supply and demand. The personal tie between employer and employed was replaced by a purely cash nexus. Social security became less important than unfettered individual enterprise. Expansion was so rapid, there was no time to think. The revolution was as thoughtless as a river in flood. It swept away the Elizabethan code of wages and apprenticeship as antiquated and irrational. Instead it supplemented inadequate wages out of the rates, thus turning workmen into state-fed paupers. And it provoked urgent new problems of crowding, hygiene, hours of work and the employment of women and children, which it made no attempt to solve.

And the state did nothing. It didn't think it was its business. Nor did the best brains in the country. They defended this *laissez-faire* attitude on the score, if you please, of freedom. Economists wanted Freedom of Contract and Freedom of Trade. The political philosophers defined Liberty as "a man's right to do as he wills". All law is therefore contrary to liberty. But a certain amount of law is unavoidable. What then is the justification of a law?—Its usefulness. What is useful?—That which makes us happy. What is happiness?—Pleasure. What is pleasure?—Every-one knows what gives him pleasure. In short: "Every man knows best what is best for himself." That is the catch-phrase of these Utilitarians, as they were called.

Very simple. But you see the fallacy. They con-founded *quantity* with *quality*. A man may know what gives him pleasure, but, if the pleasure is of a low order, like a bottle of whisky for breakfast, it can't be said to be best for him. It's like saying that the survival of the fittest is the same thing as the survival of the best. And, indeed, Darwin's theory of Evolution *was* used by some as an argument against state interference. But the survival of the fittest only means that in any given surroundings, good or bad, those best suited to them will survive. If you and I and a cockroach were put to live in a sewer, you and I might die before the cockroach, because in the circumstances the cockroach was fittest to survive. But I wouldn't say—would *you*?—that the cockroach was the best of us three.

This fallacy was corrected by a later Utilitarian, John Stuart Mill. By utility, he said, he meant "utility in the *largest* sense, grounded on the *permanent* interests of man, regarded as a *progressive* being". In other words, pleasure, liberty, usefulness were not to be estimated by their *quantity*, but by their *quality*. But that knocked the bottom out of the Utilitarian philosophy. In fact it pointed the way to a new philosophy, which began to take shape soon afterwards. T. H. Green was one of its first exponents. In 1880, he defined freedom as "the power of men to make the best of themselves". Obviously, if the state was to ensure freedom in *that* sense—if it was to provide all its citizens with the power to make the best of themselves—quite a lot of interference would be necessary.

By 1880, then, the tide of opinion was turning.

Indeed, a number of Factory Acts had already been passed. Bit by bit the state extended its authority over hours of work and the safety of workers. And at the turn of the century it was tentatively tackling the problems of wages and of insurance against accident, sickness and unemployment.

Meanwhile capitalism itself was changing. The provision of capital for business was made much easier by the formation of limited liability joint-stock companies in the second half of the nineteenth century. The comparatively small capitalist undertaking owned and managed by one or two individuals was replaced by great industrial concerns owned by numerous shareholders and managed by their elected directors. The lot of the worker seemed harder than ever. His individual bargaining power with the old factory owner had been feeble enough. Against these new combines he was powerless—*unless he, too, combined with his fellows*. Combinations of workers were made illegal at first, partly on the specious ground that they interfered with the individual worker's freedom of contract. But nothing could stop them. And, in spite of opposition and legal restrictions, Trade Unions grew in strength, till the great combinations of capital were opposed by equally great combinations of labour.

A free fight ensued of unlimited rounds: Capital *versus* Labour, with the state holding the Ring. So it had been at the beginning of the Industrial Revolution, and so it was just before the War. But there was a difference. In the palmy days of *laissez-faire* the struggle had been an indiscriminate, all-in mêlée, without any rules. It was no concern of the state whether one side was armed, so to speak, with crowbars and the other with toothpicks, or who was knocked out and trampled on. But now the fight was between two well-organised forces; there *were* certain rules; and the state felt a certain responsibility to see fair play. It even blew the whistle of legislation if there was too conspicuous a foul.

Then came the War. The state had all at once to interfere with economic life to an unprecedented extent. And since war requirements are totally different from peace requirements, the entire economic structure was distorted and warped. When peace came, government hastened to unburden itself of its emergency responsibilities. But it couldn't do so completely. The state had upset the national economy; the state must put it right. And all sorts of new problems were arising as a *result* of the War: violent fluctuations in prices, loss or disturbance of foreign markets, decay of old trades in some parts of the country and rise of new trades in other parts. Depressions, unrest, strikes—these were the consequences. Reorganisation was essential, but impossible without government help and guidance. What form did it take?

Well, it actively fostered still further concentrations of capital and labour. Prosperity, said the experts, depended on the elimination of waste. If every industry were organised as a unit, if it took united action under unified control, waste would be eliminated, output would be raised, costs would be lowered. So encouragement was given—and sometimes more than encouragement—to larger amalgamations in Cotton, Coal, Iron and Steel, Agricultural Marketing, Shipping and so on. But rationalisation led to something like monopoly. And monopolies may threaten the interests of the consumer. So state supervision was necessary even after reorganisation had taken place.

Public utility concerns, of course, call for even more supervision. So gas companies, electricity undertakings, railways, the B.B.C., the Port of London Authority, the Bank of England and such like, have all been made subject in varying degrees to public control.

But the tendency towards socialisation in big industries is noticeable even apart from government encouragement. In the old days the capitalist had been both owner and manager of the factory. With the advent of joint-stock companies, ownership and management were divorced. Ownership is distributed among an enormous number of shareholders who leave the management of their capital to paid officials. The effect is twofold. First, capital is to some extent democratised. Instead of one big capitalist owning the whole concern, you have thousands of small capitalists each owning a fraction of it. Take the Big Five Banks as an example. In 1927, their capital was sixty million, and there were about 275,000 shareholders. The holding of these "capitalists" averaged out at £220 a head. Secondly, in the biggest enterprises, at any rate, stability and reputation tend to become more important than large profits. The number of shareholders is enormous, but beyond an annual meeting they have nothing to do with the management. They are, so to speak, "the public" rather than "the owners". Policy and management are in the hands of experts of a new type who tend to regard their responsibility as a public one. Dividends must be adequate. But good management, good reserves, good wages, and good products—these are their chief concern.

Labour, too, was encouraged to organise. The assistance rendered to government in industrial administration by Labour leaders during the War had put the Unions on almost an official basis. Collective bargaining now seemed the best means to industrial peace. So in trades where labour was already highly organised, either Joint Councils were set up representative of associations of employers and workers, or existing machinery was strengthened by statute—as in the case of the Railways in 1921 and the Cotton Industry in 1934. And for trades in which no adequate organisation existed, the Trade Boards Act of 1918 provided the necessary wage-fixing machinery. By 1929 some eight million workers were covered in this way.

These measures do not, it is true, give the workers any share in the control of their industry. Even in the matter of wages they do no more than suggest that payment for labour of various kinds may be after all not a matter to be decided in an unrestricted competitive market, but a problem of distributing justly the total earnings of the concern. But they do seem to me to point the way to a new conception of the whole problem of capital and labour. The *old* idea was: Capital *versus* Labour—a free fight, and no quarter. And, goodness knows, strikes and lock-outs as a method of settling disputes are as irrational and barbarous as war between nations or duels between individuals. The *new* idea, however faintly conceived as yet, seems to envisage capital and labour in each industry jointly regulating that industry through their representatives sitting in Common

Council. We may even go further and foresee a time when, on the analogy of the state, the Management will be the Executive and the Joint Council the Legislature of the industry.

But where does the state come in? What are its functions? That question is usually put in another form. How *far* should the state intervene? Where should state control stop? But that seems to me a rather old-fashioned way of stating the problem. It implies that state control and private enterprise are incompatible, or, at least, antagonistic. Capital and Labour were similarly regarded as eternal enemies; and later on we shall see that there is much the same attitude towards freedom in general: The Free Man *versus* the State; Capital *versus* Labour; Private Enterprise *versus* State Control. Isn't that way of looking at things rather out of date? It's not a question, surely, which shall beat and boss the other, but of making each couple work together for the benefit of both of them and all of us.

Therefore it seems to me pointless to draw a line and say to the state, as old King Canute said to the tide: "Thus far and no farther", and equally unhelpful to beg the question the other way and say that the state should own, control and run everything. State socialism was the nineteenth-century answer to *laissez-faire*. *Laissez-faire* is dead and buried. And with all respect I suggest that state socialism of the orthodox doctrinaire type is a venerable but anti-quated survival from a previous age. It has served its purpose. And now twentieth-century problems need twentieth-century solutions.

So, surely, it isn't a question of defining arbitrarily the limits of state interference, but of indicating the spheres in which at any given time the state can usefully function. And at the moment these seem to be fairly obvious. In the sphere of industry, the state should continue to encourage the semi-socialisation of industry and the harmonious collaboration of capital and labour on joint councils, on the lines already indicated. It should further see that the policy of the industry furthers not only its own sectional interests but those of the whole nation. Outside that sphere the state should tackle all those problems that no one else *can* tackle—for instance, education, un-employment, sickness, old age, pauperism, housing, public health, and so on.

If you ask me where all this leads to, I must answer that nobody can ever tell anybody that. But certain tendencies do seem pretty clear. It looks as though we were heading towards the organisation of trades and industries into self-governing units subject to the legislative sovereignty of parliament and the executive supervision of the government. It looks as though all members of an industry would have a voice in its government, as all citizens do in the government of the state. And it looks as though the remuneration appropriate to every form of work would be determined on the principle of a just distribution of total earnings. That at any rate would be one way of reconciling those three essentials—Economic Efficiency, Social Justice and Individual Liberty. And it isn't so very different, notice, from the mediaeval theory of Just Price.

All this, of course, is a long way off. And the way isn't smooth or easy. We have to tackle sectional and selfish interests. Not all industry has as yet a social conscience; in some professions the reward of individual enterprise is out of all proportion to its social value; and there are still a large number of people who are ignorant of, or indifferent to, the very existence of a social problem at all.

Moreover, there is this terrible danger of modern Nationalism. Instead of living together harmoniously and trading one with another like men in civilised society, each nation wants to make itself self-sufficient and live in isolation like a primitive man in his cave. So that every nation has too much of one thing and too little of another, and each lives in fear that his neighbour will come and take what he wants and more. And millions and millions have to be spent on armaments for defence that might have been spent on creating human happiness.

I read once somewhere of a prehistoric monster—I think it was some kind of Dinosaur. Anyway it was eighty feet long and weighed about thirty-five tons. Its brain, on the other hand, measured four inches by two by one. It was covered from head to tail with horny scales and bony plates. Still it didn't feel safe. So from generation to generation it grew more armour and thicker, till it couldn't see out of its eyes or open its mouth. Then it was perfectly safe—but dead of starvation.

If we take it as a warning, it will not have died in vain.

VIII

OUR CIVIL LIBERTIES

So far we've been discussing how we got our Freedom.
It's now time to discuss what our Freedom is. If you
refer to an ordinary text-book, you will probably find
a section devoted to something called "The Liberty
of the Subject". And the section will have a number
of subheadings. The wording of these varies slightly
in different books, but they all mean the same thing,
and we can sum them up as Personal Freedom,
Freedom of Expression and Freedom of Assembly and
Association.

The Liberty of the Subject, then, what does it
amount to?

It's a little disappointing at the outset to find that
there's no such thing. At least no such thing is
expressly stated in our laws. Perhaps that's not quite
true of Personal Liberty, because there is a clause
in Magna Carta which says that no man shall be
arrested or imprisoned except by lawful judgment
of his peers or by the law of the land. But that
stated a principle; it didn't confer a new right. And,

if it comes to principles, we've already seen that it is a principle of the Rule of Law that no man can be made to suffer except for a breach of the law legally proved in an ordinary court of law. But the principle is true, not because any law states it as a fact, but because the law provides a remedy for its breach. In fact, it provides several remedies. If anyone unlawfully takes away your personal liberty—in plain words, imprisons you—the Writ of Habeas Corpus, of which I've already spoken, will get you free. You can then bring an action for damages for false imprisonment and you can also prosecute the person who imprisoned you for assault.

So you can only lose your liberty if you break the law. But the law in places is very brittle, not to say indefinite, so that it very often rests with a policeman to say whether or not you have broken it. We've all heard of such offences as "obstructing the police in the execution of their duty" and "using insulting words and behaviour". Two people recently were accused of "obstructing the police", one of them for saying (quite correctly) to a constable "You have no legal authority to confiscate that property", and the other for accompanying the first man to the police station as a witness. And some years ago an unemployed man was fined for using those insulting words: "Give us bread". I quote these instances from publications of the National Council for Civil Liberties, from whom, if you are interested, you can get any amount of information on the subject.

But it's the principle of the thing I'm concerned with, and that principle is best illustrated in a story by Anatole France. I am speaking from memory and I may have got some of the details wrong. But anyway, a man made his living by selling vegetables from a barrow. He had done so all his life; he was a well-known character locally and much respected. One day, as he was trundling his barrow, a policeman held up the traffic. The man didn't see or hear and overstepped the mark. The policeman would accept no excuses and arrested him. Next day he appeared in court and was completely bewildered. He heard the policeman give evidence in an official rigmarole, the French equivalent of "acting on information received". Prisoner had obstructed him and used insulting words. He had said to him "Mort aux vaches!"—Death to the cows! The man had really said no such thing. Nor was the policeman wilfully committing perjury. But "Death to the cows!" was his particular formula for anything said to him by people he arrested. Well, the poor man went to prison. When he came out he once more trundled his barrow. But no one would buy. He was a gaol-bird. People shouted things after him, and small boys pelted him with refuse. He had lost his character and his livelihood. What was to be done? Only one thing—go back to prison. He knew how to do that. So, seeing a policeman up a side-street, he left his barrow and went up to him. "Mort aux vaches!" he said to the policeman. Death to the cows! But this was a nice policeman. Or anyway it wasn't his formula. He merely looked hurt, "You shouldn't have said that", he replied. And there the story ends.

There is another offence called "frequenting or loitering in a public place with intent to commit a felony". Let the figures speak for themselves. In 1930, 2398 people were arrested on this charge. In 1934, the number was 4834. In four years the numbers had doubled. And of the 4834 charges made in 1934, no fewer than 1449—that is between a third and a quarter—were withdrawn or dismissed. The increase in the total is in itself alarming; the proportion withdrawn or dismissed is a bit high to be excused on the ground of "genuine mistake". Two sixteen-year old boys, returning from a shop errand, stopped to watch a game of billiards through the windows of a hall. They were arrested and charged. The case was dismissed. But should it have been brought?

Other police practices need careful watching. For instance, the practice in certain police forces of making arrests on suspicion and keeping the arrested persons in "detention", while the police decide whether a charge shall be brought. Such detention is, I believe, illegal. The Report of the Royal Commission of 1929 drew attention to this. "You must come with me to the police station" is another abuse. Said Lord Chief Justice Hewart in an Assize Court case to a Superintendent: "What is the difference in saying you must come with me to the police station and arresting her?...In my opinion it was a most improper procedure...And", he added, "I hope this will be a lesson."

And what about the alleged statements of prisoners? As a judge remarked some years ago, "the atmosphere of a police station seems to be singularly conducive to confessions". And the Royal Commission suggested that "many of the voluntary statements now tendered in court are not 'voluntary' in the strict sense of the word". Again, it is a principle of English justice that a man is presumed to be innocent till the contrary is proved. Is this always true in Petty Sessional Courts? You know the two old chestnuts about magistrates. "If you hadn't 'a done summat", said one to the defendant, "you wouldn't 'a been here". "We gave him a month", said another afterwards, "but, if we'd been *sure* he was guilty, we'd have given him six".

But that raises the subject of freedom in relation to justice, which I shall deal with later.[1] Let me pass on now to Freedom of Expression.

There is no legal right to Freedom of Expression. Neither Freedom of Speech, nor Freedom of Discussion, nor Freedom of Publication, nor Liberty of the Press—all of which are included in Freedom of Expression—are to be found in any statute or among the maxims of the Common Law. What we call our rights in these respects are based on exactly the same principle as personal freedom: No man can be made to suffer except for a breach of the law. So Freedom of Expression boils down to this. Anyone can say, write or print anything he likes, provided he *doesn't* say, write or print anything he *mayn't* say, write or print. Very well then, what mayn't we say, write or print? That depends on whether we are expressing our opinion about individuals, or government, or religion and morals.

To take individuals first. If we *say* anything untrue and defamatory about anyone else, we may be sued for damages for slander. Most of us make ourselves liable several times a day. If we write or print it, we may be sued in a civil action for damages or be prosecuted criminally for libel. And not only we who wrote it, but, if it's printed, the printer, the publisher

[1] See Talk IX.

as well, and anyone who sells a copy, anyone who, having read a copy, passes it on to someone else, and even, perhaps, anyone who reads it aloud. Honest belief in its truth is no excuse. Even truth itself is only an excuse if we can prove that it's in the public interest that the truth should be known.

A journalist once composed an imaginary article, entitled "Motor-Mad Dieppe", to illustrate the gaiety of Englishmen abroad. In it he wrote: "There is Artemus Jones with a woman who is not his wife.... You would not suppose by his goings on that he was a churchwarden at Peckham." Unfortunately there happened to be an Artemus Jones. He had never been to Dieppe; he was a bachelor; he was not a churchwarden; and he did not live in Peckham. Nevertheless he sued for libel and got £1760.[1] That, I imagine, is an extreme case. Borderline cases occur more frequently in literary, dramatic, musical or artistic criticism. The rule, as far as there is one, appears to be that candid criticism must not be used as a veil for personal censure. Obviously the line is hard to draw. In old days, critics got away with a lot.

Shelley believed that Keats's death was brought about mainly by the cruel attacks of his reviewers. Thomas Carlyle described Charles Lamb as a "pitiful, rickety, gasping, staggering Tom-fool". He called

[1] Ernst and Lindey, *Hold Your Tongue!*

Coleridge "a weak, diffusive, weltering, ineffectual man", and Herbert Spencer "the most unending ass in Christendom". Ruskin, criticising some paintings by Whistler, wrote: "I have seen and heard much of Cockney impudence before now; but never expected to hear a Coxcomb ask two hundred guineas for flinging a pot of paint in the public's face." Whistler sued him. The jury gave him one farthing's damages.[1] Obviously they thought it was technically a libel, but shared Ruskin's views of Whistler's paintings. But suppose, instead of Whistler, the plaintiff had been one of the popular painters of the time. Wouldn't the damages have been real and heavy?

However, that raises questions into which we cannot go. Critics on the whole are milder nowadays, but they do sometimes use their criticism as a vent for personal animosity, and they are not often prosecuted, partly owing to the unpredictable behaviour of juries, and partly because it is bad policy for an author, composer or artist to bring an action against a critic in almost any circumstances.

If you are expressing yourself about the government, you mustn't say, write or print anything with a seditious intention—that is, an intention to bring into hatred or contempt the King, Government, Constitution, or either House of Parliament, or to

[1] *Ibid.* pp. 76–77, 104–106.

155

excite subjects to attempt to alter anything in Church or State otherwise than by lawful means, or to promote ill-will between different classes of subjects. It is also a misdemeanour to speak or publish words defamatory of any Court of Justice, or of the administration of the law therein. You see how strict the law is. And in old days, of course, any criticism of the government was regarded as sedition. Nowadays you can say almost anything about prominent politicians. They're used to it. Besides, they can't afford to be too touchy because they are dependent on public opinion. But judges aren't. So you must be much more careful with them. Still, practically speaking, in spite of the severity of the law, any criticism made in good faith with the object of reform is safe from prosecution. At least, I hope so—for my own sake.

About religion and morals the law in the past has been still more severe. For any person brought up as a Christian to deny the truth of Christianity or the authority of the Scriptures is, I believe, by statute still a criminal offence. But judges in recent decisions have taken a much more lenient view. In 1883 Lord Coleridge held that "if the decencies of controversy are observed, even the fundamentals of religion may be attacked". And perhaps the modern doctrine may best be summed up in the words of a judgment of 1908: "A man is free to speak and to teach what he pleases as to religious matters, though not as to morals;...but if, for the sake of argument, he were making a scurrilous attack on doctrines which the majority of people hold to be true, in a public place where passers-by may have their ears offended, and where young persons may come, he will render himself liable to the law of blasphemous libel."[1]

Such is the law. But in every individual case the question arises: "Is it, or is it not, a libel?" And the answer rests with a jury. So, as Dicey put it: "Freedom of discussion is in England little else than the right to write or say anything which a jury, consisting of twelve shopkeepers, think it expedient should be said or written."

The Freedom of the Press is in general no greater than the freedom of the individual in this respect, but it has in the course of time secured certain privileges with regard to fair and accurate reports of proceedings in Parliament, the Courts of Law, public meetings and so on, and in actions for libel it has also one or two advantages. It isn't, however, satisfied. According to pressmen, nearly all libel actions brought against newspapers arise out of genuine mistakes which cannot be guarded against. And I gather that a bill to amend the law has recently been presented to Parliament. On the other hand, Freedom of the Press is already

[1] Thomas and Bellot, *Leading Cases in Constitutional Law*, p. 313.

157

wide enough to admit of certain abuses—intrusion on private grief, for instance, sensationalism and prurience. One can't blame the law for that. One can't altogether blame the newspapers. At least part of the blame rests with the bad taste of the public.

Notice that books and newspapers are published without licence, while plays by law, and films by voluntary arrangement, have to be licensed. Whether and by whom they should be licensed is a good subject for debate, but rather outside our scope, as long as the censorship is not tyrannically exercised. Occasionally a work of art is banned, as Ibsen's *Ghosts* was long ago, or, to cite a more recent instance, *Green Pastures*— though the film version may now be shown. The rule, too, by which no member of the Royal Family may be impersonated on the stage till he or she has been dead for three—or is it four?—generations, nor apparently any other person, if any of the descendants object, that rule may occasion hardships. But I don't think the liberty of the subject can be said to suffer very seriously as things are, and a censorship may be preferable to the alternative risks of prosecution of author, management and actors. I leave it to you.

Freedom of Expression may be violated, however, in other more reprehensible ways. Here are two examples. The government, in its capacity of post-master, has always possessed the right to open letters.

This seems to me quite indefensible in normal times and might lead to very serious interference with individual freedom. Still, it would be legal. An example of illegal interference occurred in 1935 when, at the Air Displays at Hendon, Mildenhall and Duxford, the police confiscated pacifist literature which harmless people were selling or distributing in a perfectly orderly manner. In a case brought before the Cambridge County Court it was held that the police had exceeded their powers, though only nominal damages of a pound were awarded against them.

Now we come to the right of Assembly, or Public Meeting. Again, no such right is known to the law of England. It is merely an extension of the individual right of every subject to go where he pleases and say what he pleases, provided he doesn't go anywhere where he mayn't go, or say anything that he mayn't say. We've just seen that he may say anything that isn't seditious, blasphemous, defamatory or obscene. He can also go anywhere where it's not illegal to go. Smith can, Jones can; so can Robinson, and so can all the people in the Telephone Directory. But they mustn't trespass or cause an obstruction or a nuisance.

By custom or rule certain places like Hyde Park are habitually used for public meetings. But the law doesn't, generally speaking, provide special places for the purpose. You've got to find one. You can't, for instance, hold a meeting in the public highway, because you would obstruct it. But you have the right to pass and repass on the highway. Hence the right to hold processions. A procession cannot be prohibited in advance.[1] If a Chief Constable apprehends a breach of the peace, he must apply to a magistrate to have the organisers bound over. But the police have certain powers to regulate the routes of processions.

But suppose you have found a place to which there's no legal objection. Will your meeting now be lawful? Well, the law isn't altogether too clear, but I think the truth is this. It won't be lawful, if the *object* for which it is held is to commit a breach of the peace or to incite others to do so ; nor if the *manner* of holding it threatens a breach of the peace or causes other people reasonably to fear one. But it won't be unlawful just because it *may* excite unlawful opposition from other people, *unless the meeting offers provocation.* Thus, when the Salvation Army met at Weston-super-Mare with the knowledge that they would be opposed by some people calling themselves the Skeleton Army, their meeting was perfectly lawful, because they were inoffensive people.[2] But when

[1] This is no longer true. See note 1, p. 162.
[2] Beatty *v.* Gillbanks (1882).

160

Mr Wise, a fiery Protestant, used insulting and provocative language about Roman Catholics in a public place where there was a large Roman Catholic population, his meeting became unlawful.[1]

The next thing we want to find out is what powers the authorities possess with regard to public meetings. Well, a meeting, if otherwise lawful, cannot be prohibited in advance, just because it may provoke a breach of the peace. But once a meeting has begun, if it becomes unlawful for any of the reasons just mentioned, it can be dispersed, by force, if necessary, and every person taking part in it may be prosecuted for misdemeanour. That is the law as regards unlawful assemblies. But the authorities have an alternative way of proceeding. If even a lawful meeting has begun, or is about to begin, the police can stop or prevent it, if the officer in charge reasonably fears that a breach of the peace will occur. And anyone who disobeys can be arrested for "wilfully obstructing the police in the execution of their duty".

I rather feel that this alternative procedure is easily capable of abuse. As the *New Statesman* said of a recent case: "It appears to justify the police in prohibiting any meeting at which some speaker might in their view say something which might lead someone

[1] Wise *v.* Dunning (1902).

else to say something which might lead to a disturbance somewhere else."[1]

Freedom of Association is usually coupled with Freedom of Assembly or Public Meeting. Political Associations on a nation-wide scale began in the days of John Wilkes and formed part of the popular agitation for Parliamentary Reform. On the outbreak of the French Revolution, many of them were temporarily suppressed by Act of Parliament, but it was soon found impossible to repress movements that commanded widespread sympathy and in modern times they have been left to enjoy their Common Law rights. Petitions, too, were first extensively used about the same time and for the same purpose. The Right of Petitioning had been affirmed in the Bill of Rights after the Revolution of 1688. Apparently nowadays they are more numerous than ever. The annual average is said to be well over ten thousand.

[1] The Public Order Act, which was one of the first two Bills to receive the Royal Assent of H.M. King George VI (December 19th, 1936) has, since this Talk was delivered, modified considerably the Law of Assembly and Association. Among other things, it has made political uniforms illegal, prohibited semi-military political organisations, given the police general powers to determine the routes of processions and to prohibit *all* processions in specified areas for specified periods, subject to the consent of the local authority and of the Home Secretary, and it has made illegal the carrying of offensive weapons at political meetings.

But we don't hear much about them. Adult suffrage, the Press and the tremendous influence of public opinion in general on the government has, I suppose, reduced the importance of petitioning as a method of drawing attention to grievances.

But *economic* organisations, whether of employers or workmen, for joint action to regulate conditions of labour, were on a very different footing. At Common Law they were conspiracies in restraint of trade, and the history of Trade Unions is the story of spasmodic modifications of Common Law by statute. To begin with, statutes reinforced the Common Law. Trade Unions were unlawful associations, and anyone who joined one or helped to organise a strike was a criminal. Then, in 1825, Trade Unions were put on the borderline of the law. They were no longer illegal, but they had no legal status, and any strike might still in practice be treated as a criminal conspiracy. Between 1871 and 1876 were passed several statutes, collectively known as the Charter of Trade Unionism. The Unions ceased to be criminally liable. And in 1906 they were relieved of civil liability. Finally in 1927, as a result of the General Strike of the previous year, certain kinds of strikes were defined and made illegal, and the criminal liability of Unions in such cases was restored.

From the point of view of liberty, the problem of

Trade Unions is the problem of reconciling their right of combined action with individual freedom and the authority of the state. The problem is so formidable that it is not altogether surprising that it has, as far as possible, been shirked. When crises have arisen, too urgent to be ignored, legislation has been passed to patch up the immediate trouble, but neither government authority nor Trade Unions themselves have shown any desire for an exhaustive definition of their powers and responsibilities. Policy took the easier course of regarding them as far as possible as voluntary associations whose internal concerns and public policy were no more the business of the state than the private arrangements of a social club.[1]

And yet, you know, Trade Unions have long outgrown such an anomalous position. They are probably the most powerful social force in the state. They can keep a man out of a job. They can limit entry to a trade. They can control output. They have immense powers over their members, which are capable of being used tyrannically. They administer poor men's savings. They can make industrial agreements and break them. They can inflict hardship on the community to further their own ends. They can

[1] Ramsay Muir, *Trade Unionism and the Trade Union Bill*, p. 32.

stop public services. A legitimate strike in one trade may throw thousands out of employment in another, may ruin some firms beyond recovery, may affect adversely the prosperity of the whole nation. Their leaders hold important positions in our social machinery. They are consulted by government in times of dispute; they are spokesmen for the workers before Courts of Inquiry. They sit, as representatives of the workers, on government committees and commissions. They have an official share in state administration—under the Trade Boards Act—on wage boards, in National Insurance and on Local Employment Committees. It seems odd that bodies with such terrific powers for good or ill should, legally speaking, be so uncontrolled.

And here's another question that I think ought to be raised. Trade Unions, it will be agreed, are a tremendous social force, and their leaders perform officially important social functions. Yet the Unions are officially tied to one political party. And it is at least debatable whether institutions which have attained to such an important public status ought not to be as politically impartial as the Civil Service or the great public utility companies.

These, then, are our much-vaunted civil liberties: Personal Freedom, Freedom of Expression, Freedom of Assembly and Association. What do you think of them? In some people they arouse lyrical enthusiasm. Maybe you've noticed how politicians of all parties, and especially our elder statesmen, adopt a sort of old-school-tie-on-Speech-Day attitude towards them. Others, perhaps most people, are less enthusiastic. I can only say that usually, when I've heard the subject mentioned, the reaction is one of two kinds only—either a tolerant doubt best expressed as "Oh, yeah?" or a flat denial equivalent to "Nerts!"

Why is this? Well, I can give three reasons. First, it's undoubtedly due partly to the blackest ingratitude. Our civil liberties, as defined—or rather, as allowed —by law, are very great and fine. In many countries to-day civil liberties have nearly vanished altogether, and even among surviving democracies, few if any can show a better product than ours. But, as usual, we take our liberties for granted until they're interfered with, and so we don't think much of them. Secondly, many people, perhaps most, when they think of liberty, if they do at all, mean these civil liberties and nothing more. Some, if you jog their memories about religious liberty and political liberty, will say, in a rather bored way: "Oh yes, of course." But if you mention social liberty, they won't know what you mean. And I think part of the dissatisfaction with our liberty to-day is due to a feeling that civil liberties are all right as far as they go, but they don't go very far. I quite agree. They are only a part of freedom in its wider and proper sense, and other parts of our freedom are in not nearly so good a state. And, thirdly, though *according to law* our civil liberties sound good enough, do they work out well in practice? Aren't there, perhaps, other laws which indirectly restrict our freedom? And what about the Law Courts? What about the administration of justice? Do these protect our freedom properly? Let's see.

IX

FREEDOM AND JUSTICE

NOT long ago, I heard one of the speakers in
Hyde Park describe how he first came to London.
He had walked from Manchester in search of a job.
He arrived one evening penniless, so he asked a
policeman where he could get a night's rest. This is
his account of what happened:

"The copper put his hand in his pocket and brought
out something small and round. I thought it was
half-a-dollar. But it was only a ticket really with an
address on it. Well, I went there. They took me in,
opened a door and said, 'You're number 46.' There
were 240 beds in that room. By the time I found
mine, it was time to get up again. I complained in
the morning.

'There was a dead flea in my bed,' I said.

'A *dead* flea!' they said. 'Then why worry?'

'It wasn't the dead one that worried me,' I said.
'It was all the others coming to the funeral.'

So next night I decided to sleep out, and I was
just walking along the street, when up came a couple
of coppers.

"'Ullo,' they sez.

Well, mind you, we hadn't been introduced. But, when you're poor, you can't be too particular, so I sez:

"'Ullo, Twins,' I sez.

'What you doing?' sez one.

'I'm looking for somewhere to sleep,' I sez.

'Oh,' sez the other, 'we'll find you somewhere to sleep all right.' And they took me to the Police Station. Next morning, I was brought up before the beak. He was eighty-five years old.

'Is what the policeman says true?' He asked me.

'No,' I said.

The beak put his hand to his ear: 'What did he say?'

'He said *Yes*,' shouted the copper what stood near him.

'Oh,' said the beak, 'very well. Two pounds or sixteen days.'

'Thanks very much,' I said. 'I'll take the two pounds.'"

Now we needn't believe a word of that story. But, rightly or wrongly, that man thought he had a grievance. And I want you to notice the nature of that grievance. According to him, he was without work and without livelihood; society made very poor provision for him; he was arrested merely for loitering; the magistrate was old and deaf; the court was under police influence; the hearing of his case was a farce; he was asked to pay a fine he couldn't possibly pay; and, although he had done nothing wrong, he was sent to prison. Yet, according to my last talk, he was a free man in a free country in full possession of all his civil liberties.

There must be some mistake surely. Let's see.

In my fifth talk I said that Freedom in relation to the law meant two things. With one I dealt at the time. The second meaning was that "the laws are consistent with freedom and the processes of law protect that freedom". That's what I want to discuss now.

The law has been described as "the perfection of reason". Somebody else called it "an ass". If we had time to go fully into the subject, we should probably arrive at a compromise. But there are certain laws to which the second definition seems more apt than the first. Take the laws based on some moral principle which doesn't command the respect of large numbers of people—laws, for instance, about Sunday Observance, Licensing, Divorce, Gaming and Betting.

If man and wife both want to break off their marriage, they mustn't agree to do so. One of them has to do, or pretend to do, something morally wrong. And for six months after a decree has been obtained, both parties are at the mercy of spies and even, apparently, of anonymous letters. The result is, as Lord Snell pointed out in 1933, that there are nearly two million married people living apart. And this supposedly moral law is an incentive to subterfuge, perjury and immorality.

Again; if you play cards for small stakes in a railway carriage, you are a rogue and a vagabond and may be punished as such. If you bet—well, let me quote the author of a book called *English Justice*. "To bet with a bookmaker at his office over the telephone is legal, but to go to that office to make the bet is a serious offence.... To bet in a club is legal, to bet in a pub is a crime. If I live next door to a bookmaker, I may safely post him a letter containing a bet, but if I hand him the same letter over the hedge we are both committing an offence."[1]

Laws such as these bring the law itself into contempt, because they do not square with most people's ideas of right and wrong. Nor are they easy to enforce. Some are not enforced at all. Boxing contests, for instance, as at present conducted, are, I believe, illegal. But since the Driscoll *versus* Moran fight was stopped in 1911, they have not actually been inter-

[1] "Solicitor", *English Justice*, p. 215.

fered with. But whether such laws *shall* be enforced or not depends very largely on the police. Such a wide discretion is a burden to them and a danger to the community.

On the one hand, the police may be over-zealous. There was a recent case in the provinces. A police constable, having written letters from a false address to a hotel where a club was registered, took up residence. He was asked to sign the register and to fill in a membership form for the club. Other police officers and a policewoman, who said she was a school-teacher, joined him for dinner. They had sherry, gin and limes, champagne and brandy. When the premises were raided, the only people in the bar were the police officers and the policewoman. And an inspector testified that he believed the club to have been quiet and well conducted. But it was struck off the register and the proprietor was fined.

On the other hand, the police may think it better not to do more than is absolutely necessary. There may be an occasional raid or round-up just to show that the law is the law, but the individual officer, if he's a decent chap, isn't going to court unnecessary unpopularity. Live and let live, will be his motto. But just think what appalling temptation he is exposed to. You may remember the Liverpool cases of 1927, the Goddard case in 1929, the Sheffield cases in 1930. But I don't want to cite exceptional cases, I only want to point out the general danger. Let us, on the analogy of Hogarth's Rake's Progress, imagine a similar Policeman's Progress. First Tableau: a cherubic policeman good-naturedly closes his eyes as a street-bookie takes a bet. Second Tableau: a shame-faced policeman accepts a tip for continuing to close his eyes. Third Tableau: a sinister policeman demands a tip to keep his eyes closed. Fourth Tableau: a brutal policeman threatens, unless tipped, to prosecute. And what about the finale? A Court scene, do you think, with the magistrate sentencing the bookie and warmly commending a now perfectly fiendish policeman for his zeal? Or do you prefer a happy ending? A conscience-stricken policeman on his knees in floods of tears restoring to the bookie his ill-gotten gains?

The trouble is we have not only some bad laws, but too many laws—more than any other nation. We think of Parliament as the Legislature, but Parliament only makes a fraction of the laws that govern us. I've already dealt with the immense number of Regulations made by government departments. But besides the law of the Legislature and the law of the Executive, there is also the law of the Judiciary— Common Law. The bulk of our private laws, that is the law between citizen and citizen, has been made by judges in the Law Courts. And the amount of it! The *English and Empire Digest* cites a quarter of a million cases, and the *Annual Digest* adds a thousand new cases every year. Any of these precedents may be quoted in Court.

Yet cases occur for which no precedents exist; all precedents are not good precedents; many are contradictory; and some, though hopelessly antique, may still be valid. But all Common Law, good or bad, is made at the expense of individuals. You go to law to establish your legal rights. But the decision in your case may make new law, and it's you who will have to pay for that new law, perhaps in several stages of appeal up to the House of Lords. In short, do you want to know what the law is? Then, to quote a famous old lawyer:[1] "Wait until your fortune has been spent in the enquiry, and you *will* know."

Judge-made law has the advantage of elasticity. It grows to meet new needs. But it has become overgrown and tangled, and the weeding comes out of the pockets of private litigants. The obvious remedy is to reduce both Statute and Common Law to a code. But that's not easy. There's such a mass of both. And the very statutes that codify bits of it need themselves to be interpreted in the Courts and

[1] Jeremy Bentham.

174

so lead to yet more case law. Still, codification has been attempted with success in some sections of law, and the process could be continued almost indefinitely. But who is to do it? Parliament has neither the time, the inclination nor the knowledge. And as for lawyers doing it—well, to quote Sir William Harcourt: "You might just as well expect a man to lift himself up in a basket as ask the lawyers by themselves to reform the law." But mightn't Parliament appoint a commission under the Lord Chancellor to take the matter permanently in hand?

Now let's turn to the processes of law. We have, we are told, "the best law in the world". If so, it's better than most of us can afford. As the London Chamber of Commerce said in its 1930 Report: "It is as if a person who wished to buy a cheap car were told that he could only have a Rolls or a Daimler."

To go to law in England costs more than in any country in Europe. To the majority of the nation that cost is prohibitive, and to the remainder the cost often exceeds the benefits obtained. Procedure, both before and during trial, is exceedingly complicated. The book of the rules alone contains 2500 pages. Owing to unbusiness-like methods, time and money are wasted by parties waiting for their case to be called. The rules of evidence are so strict and formal that the minutest proof is often necessary even for facts not really in dispute. Appeals are a form of legal gambling. The party unsuccessful in the lower Court bets double or quits on the decision of the superior Court. And notice that when the judge in the lower Court is overruled, it is the private litigant who pays for his mistake. Here are two examples quoted from Mr Claud Mullins's book *In Quest of Justice*.

A lady renting a cottage at £3. 12s. 0d. a month claimed protection under the Rent Acts. She lost her case in the County Court. She won it in the High Court. She lost it again in the Court of Appeal. That cost her £165. Two and a half years later she was still trying to pay it off in instalments.

The other case was a claim for £40,000 against underwriters. It went up and up till it reached the House of Lords. The costs of one side only were £89,000.

So you see you can still be heavily out of pocket even if you win. A vicar once refused to administer the Sacrament to his churchwarden, because the churchwarden didn't believe in the devil. That case, too, went to the House of Lords, and the churchwarden won. But, remarked the judge, the churchwarden would probably believe in the devil all right as soon as he got his lawyer's bill. As Mr Justice

Mathew once said: "In this country justice is open to all—like the Ritz Hotel."

The result is that the public is kept away from the Courts. The business community in London have succeeded in obtaining a cheap and efficient Commercial Court and still cheaper, and apparently more satisfactory, Arbitration Courts presided over by laymen. But elsewhere, as the Chamber of Commerce reported, people "will go any length to avoid going into Court". Business communities have developed tribunals of their own; compulsory arbitration clauses are a common feature of modern contracts; the growth of administrative Courts run by government officials is itself almost entirely a result of the clumsiness and expense of Common Law machinery. One wonders if even lawyers profit by it. The uncertainty of the law may increase the number of potential lawsuits, but the cost of lawsuits prevents the bringing of all but the absolutely unavoidable.

A drastic reduction in the cost of litigation is imperative. That again is easier said than done. Some maintain that justice can never be cheap, because ascertaining facts is an expensive business. But, first, the facts are not always in dispute; secondly, what is possible in the Commercial Court should be possible in other Courts as well; and, thirdly, justice is much cheaper abroad. Anyway, a good deal could be done straight away to simplify procedure and proof.

So far I have only spoken of the higher central Courts. What about provincial justice? Well, the first thing that strikes one is that in the higher branches there isn't enough of it. There are the Assize Courts to be sure, but the visiting judge is not familiar with local conditions. The original basis of the Assizes was a combination of London judge and local jury. But now that the jury is fast disappearing in civil cases, the element of local knowledge is likely to disappear also. Some say that the Assize system is anyhow invaluable, because of the tremendous impression made on the locality by the pomp and ceremony attached to the visit of the "Red Judge". There may be something in that; though in depressed areas there is evidence that the ceremonial is resented as meaningless flummery.[1] But regarded either as spectacle or as justice, the Assize system is rather expensive. And it is a moot point whether the expense involved in the travelling personnel of touring Courts wouldn't be better employed in the upkeep of permanent local Courts.

There are, of course, the permanent County Courts. These have been called the Poor Man's Courts, because their function is to provide justice in minor

[1] Charles Muir, *Justice in a Depressed Area*, p. 59.

cases without unnecessary formality or expense. Procedure hasn't in fact been simplified as much as was hoped, and the cost of litigation is often out of proportion to the sum at stake. Still these Courts have proved so successful that their work has been increased by Parliament. But at present their jurisdiction is limited to disputes of up to one hundred pounds in most cases, though in some the limit is higher. So they cannot deal with the more important types of civil cases. Yet it seems rather absurd that such cases should have to be carried to London. It must be a great handicap to big industrial centres like the Tyneside not to have competent Courts of their own. It certainly wastes time and money. What is wanted surely is a greater decentralisation of justice. One suggestion is this: Divide England and Wales into seven areas. Give each area a set of local Courts, with a procedure simplified on the lines of the London Commercial Court and with judges resident in the locality.[1] What do you think of that?

Now we come to the Petty Sessional Courts, commonly called the "Police Courts". It is important to realise what a tremendous part they play in the administration of justice. They can impose sentences up to a maximum of six months' imprisonment with hard labour, or a fine of one hundred pounds, or

[1] *Ibid.* p. 64.

both. In 1933, 38,681 people in all were sent to prison by the various Criminal Courts in the country. Of these, 33,162 were committed by magistrates. In addition they have very wide civil jurisdiction concerning matrimonial relationships, affiliation, trading, rates, tenancies, employment, licensing— in fact, most things that touch the daily life of the people. In London and some eighteen other towns, the magistrates are stipendiaries, who must have been barristers of not less than seven years' standing. Throughout the rest of the country there are about a thousand Courts with Benches of unpaid amateurs.

About the stipendiaries complaints are sometimes made that they are too old, and that they have to rush their work. But it is against the amateur magistrates that criticism is mainly directed. In the old days they were appointed from among the local gentry. Biased they undoubtedly were when their own interests were concerned. Who isn't? But they had a sense of responsibility, and their social position at least put them above intrigue or undue influence from the Clerk of the Court and the police. However, they were mostly Conservatives, so machinery was set up to redress the balance of party representation on the Bench. The result has been unfortunate. Appointments are often made on political grounds, sometimes as a reward for political services. An active party worker is a propagandist. And a propagandist mind is the very antithesis of a judicial mind.

Once a magistrate, always a magistrate. Some may leave the district, others from infirmity or apathy may cease to attend. Sometimes too many attend at once, so that they look more like a jury than a judicial Bench. Many in course of time become too old or deaf. Mr Leo Page in his book *Justice of the Peace* mentions one Bench of fourteen members, whose *average* age is well over seventy. And old people, it can't be denied, are often out of touch and sympathy with the problems and outlook of the young. As for deafness: "Eh," said a Chairman well over eighty in a case of exceeding the speed limit, "Eh, twenty-six miles an hour? But I thought it was legal up to thirty miles."—"Not twenty-six miles, sir," bellowed the police officer. "I said thirty-six."—"Oh, forty-six!" said the Chairman. "That's very different. Why didn't you speak up?"[1] One is inclined to sympathise with the officer, if not with the language of another defendant who, after being considerably bullied, said: "If you can't hear what's said, you're not blank well fit to sit there. Come and stand by me and I'll shout in your adjectival ear."[2]

[1] Leo Page, *Justice of the Peace*, pp. 253–254.
[2] "Solicitor", *English Justice*, p. 175.

These magistrates need have no knowledge of the law. For that they rely, not always satisfactorily, it is said, on their Clerk. The rules of evidence are frequently disregarded. Magistrates sometimes pick up, quite innocently, information or gossip outside the Court which may prejudice a case. "Let me tell you, sir," said a Chairman to a solicitor, "we have had a very bad report about your client."[1] The sentences they impose lack system and uniformity. The Home Secretary in 1936 drew attention to this in a circular about the treatment of motorists. But not only motorists deserve equality of treatment. The author of *English Justice* records a case where for precisely similar offences, one man was fined forty shillings, while the other got three months. When he subsequently asked why: "Oh," said the Chairman, "the evidence was much stronger in the one case than in the other."[2]

Magistrates in their ignorance come to rely unduly on the Clerk and the police. The Clerk is usually a solicitor with a local private practice. He may not practise before his own Bench, but there may be clients of his on that Bench, and other clients may appear before it on motoring or other offences. That puts him in a false position. He should surely be a

[1] "Solicitor", *English Justice*, p. 42.
[2] "Solicitor", *The Citizen and the Law*, p. 230.

whole-timer without any private practice. In Court he often overshadows the magistrates, because he alone knows the law. When this happens, he has power without responsibility.

The influence of the police over magistrates is too well known to need emphasis. The mere fact that the Petty Sessional Court is commonly called the "Police Court" is itself significant. Many magistrates behave as though the Court were actually a police department. The police themselves sometimes behave as if it were, by giving orders in Court, sitting beside the Clerk facing the body of the Court, and acting as advocates. Phrases such as "We must support our own officers", and "Are you trying to make the police out to be liars?" are quite common. In some Courts police evidence tends to be accepted blindly. Motorists know that. Poor people know it better. Bail is practically unobtainable if the police object. In 1932 a man charged with theft pleaded not guilty and asked for bail. The police objected on the ground that they had not yet recovered the stolen property and the man hadn't helped them to do so.[1]

But why go on? If you read some of the books I have mentioned you will see how much stronger than I have put it is the case against the Petty Sessional Court. What is there to be said on the other side?

[1] "Solicitor", *English Justice*, p. 54.

That there are many excellent magistrates individually and some good Benches collectively everyone will agree. But of the system as it exists to-day I do not know of a single champion, except among magistrates themselves, who occasionally write to *The Times* to say what good chaps they are. On the other hand, quite a lot of people would prefer to see the system reformed rather than abolished—partly because of its historical traditions, and partly because, to quote one of them: "That close communion of ordinary men and women with the administration of justice has results of enormous social value."[1] The reforms suggested are fairly obvious. The exclusion of political influence in the appointment of magistrates; a probationary period to start with; an age limit; exclusion of the absentees and the infirm; not more than three, or at most, five, to sit on the bench together; whole-time clerks; and somehow—but nobody suggests exactly how—the police to be prevented from exercising undue influence.

Do you think that would do the trick? In certain parts of England—rural districts, for instance—where society is still to some extent patriarchal, perhaps it would. But I can't think it would in industrialised areas. And for the life of me I can't understand how people can be expected to respect a tribunal, not one

[1] Leo Page, *Justice of the Peace*, p. 28.

184

of whose members is qualified in the law. There is one kind of administrative tribunal used to apply government Regulations which may give us a tip. It consists of a Chairman who is a lawyer and two others, one representing business interests and one with experience of working-class conditions. Mightn't we find a solution of the Petty Sessional Court problem on somewhat similar lines? Suppose the Chairman had to be qualified in the law, and there were two lay-men with him, one of whom had to have experience of working-class conditions?—There's a danger, of course, of a sort of class tug-of-war between the two laymen. That would be horrible. But is it inevitable? Think it over.

There is one type of case dealt with in these Courts that raises such important principles that I can't pass it over. It concerns the relationships of married people. I refer to Maintenance and Separation Orders. It seems to me really frightful that these intimacies should be discussed in open Court before inquisitive and perhaps sniggering neighbours. In some cases a vindictive woman takes advantage of the opportunity to hold her husband up to public ridicule. It is he then who suffers an appalling humiliation. More generally, it is a genuine case of a married couple unable to get on together. Why should they be put to such a painful ordeal? Various remedies have been suggested: that justices should hear such cases privately on special days; that Domestic Courts should be set up for the purpose; or that all matrimonial cases should be transferred to the County Courts.[1]

I must pass over Quarter Sessions and the Coroner's Court, both of which many people think might be abolished without loss. Quarter Sessions are mainly useful as a training ground for young barristers, and Coroner's Courts as an opportunity for insurance companies to get evidence and for journalists to get copy. But I have said enough by now for us to be able to tackle that hackneyed old phrase: "There is one law for the rich and another for the poor." Is there? I'm afraid there's no doubt about it.

In one sense it's inevitable. In whatever way you organise society there will always be some who will be able to wangle preferential treatment, even if it's only in their ability to secure the services of the best barristers. In another sense, the law gives preferential treatment to the poor—or at least to the *very* poor. If you possess not more than fifty pounds, or don't earn more than two pounds a week, you can, broadly speaking, litigate as much as you like with professional

[1] For a discussion of this problem see *Just Justice?* by Cecil Geeson. A Bill dealing with the subject is now (February, 1937) before Parliament.

assistance free of charge. If you lose your case, you can carry it on appeal up to the House of Lords. You've got nothing to lose, and you may gain a lot. And even if you gain nothing, you've the spiteful satisfaction of knowing that your opponent will have to pay all his costs. So, you see, though this Poor Persons' procedure is admirable in principle, it is not properly safeguarded against abuse, and its scope is so limited that in practice it helps the destitute rather than the poor.

But even poor people outside its limit can take advantage of the law. There are, it is said, certain solicitors, popularly knows as "ambulance chasers", who are not above a gamble, which some people would call blackmail. A poor man falls off a bus. It may be his own fault. "Never mind," says the solicitor. "We'll tell the company that, if they don't pay up, we'll sue them. They'll be out of pocket anyhow. It's a case of heads you win, tails they lose. Ten to one they'll pay up, and we'll go shares."

But, generally speaking, if you aren't either destitute or well off, but merely poor—well, to put it discreetly, you are not so well provided for by the law. Thus, many people are sent to prison either on remand or on default, because they can't pay money demanded of them. Poverty is their crime. When actually accused of crime, the poor man is at a disadvantage in that he can't afford one of those specialist barristers who, as everybody knows, make all the difference with a jury. The higher Courts are out of the poor man's reach. They are too expensive for him. And many matters—libel and slander cases, for instance—can only be dealt with, or at any rate started, in the High Court. So a poor man's reputation is apparently not considered as valuable as a rich man's. Even in the lowest Courts, the Petty Sessional Courts, a poor man is at a disadvantage, for it cannot be denied that an undefended man stands less chance than a defended one. Nor has he the necessary means to appeal. Again, a poor man can hardly get a divorce, for even an undefended divorce suit costs between sixty and seventy pounds. The licensing laws bear more hardly on the poor than on the rich, and the increasing number of working men's clubs is a sign of their attempt to escape the fussy interference of magistrates and police. As for the Betting Laws, even the Royal Commission of 1929 observed that "a considerable section of public opinion regards the present law as class legislation".

And what do you suppose is the poor man's attitude to all this? When he sees that the law apparently discriminates against him, he calls it class legislation. When he finds that the higher Courts are virtually closed to him and that in the lower Petty Sessional

Courts he is fobbed off with an inferior kind of justice, he puts it down to class rule and class prejudice. Matters are not improved by the fact that he and his kind—and even people familiar with him and his kind—have so little part in the administration of justice. Is that altogether wise? This is a democracy. Working men are in politics, in parliament, sometimes in the Cabinet. They hold responsible positions in industry. Some of them have built up businesses themselves. But they're not conspicuous, are they, on the Bench or at the Bar? The training is necessarily difficult: it is also expensive; and, as things are, a long time passes before that profession yields a livelihood. But is that inevitable, or merely bad management?

Many people may feel sure, and perhaps rightly, that this state of things is *not* due to class legislation, class rule, or class prejudice; that it is merely an out-of-date survival which a conservative nation has not yet bothered to reform; and that actually things are not really as bad as they seem. But, as Lord Chief Justice Hewart has so well said: "Justice should not only be done, but should manifestly be seen to be done." Otherwise respect for the law is undermined, and respect for the law is the basis of society. That dissatisfaction is very strong and real cannot be denied. Even if we discount the very serious, and sometimes alarming, generalisations and warnings published by people who speak with authority and experience, it is very difficult to avoid the conclusion that legal reform is as necessary to-day as parliamentary reform was before 1832.

As for the proper remedies, some are matters of common sense. About others, more technical, I am not competent to speak. But I have tried here and there in this talk to quote the suggestions of those who *are* competent. Reform is difficult, of course. But legal reform is not nearly as difficult as social reform. And we are at least making an effort at that. And if some tell me—as no doubt many will—what a fool I am to rush in where angels fear to tread, my answer is that, unless amateur fools like you and me do do a bit of rushing in, the only treading the expert angels will ever do is to go on marking time.

X

THE FREE MAN *VERSUS* THE STATE

WE'VE been a long time nosing and poking about in history and law, watching the several processes by which liberty is made and criticising the results piecemeal—like a party of shareholders going over their factory. Let us now review the organisation, machinery and output as a whole.

Here we are then. This is John Bull and Sons, Limited, Manufacturers of Freedom, Central Offices in Whitehall, Works and Warehouses at Westminster and in the Strand. A very old and respectable firm, ladies and gentlemen. Been in business for upwards of a thousand years. Started in quite a small way on the same site and has built up the present huge premises with branches run by relations all over the world and subordinate concerns everywhere.

Like all old institutions it is very conservative—even old-fashioned in many ways, though more in appearance than in fact. Most foreign competitors have gone into liquidation at least once in their career and started business again on entirely new lines. But John Bull likes to keep up the old traditions and preserve the old forms. Prefers to adapt the old rather than to adopt the new. Stolid common sense serves him as well in his opinion as others are served by their newfangled notions. Rather slow and expensive, perhaps, but very reliable. Not much given to advertisement. Thinks it rather vulgar. In fact, in private, he is more inclined than most to laugh at himself and even to run the old firm down. But that's not modesty so much as cocksureness. He is so convinced of the superiority of his own methods. Yes, rather smug, I'm afraid. And that's what makes him so exasperating to foreign rivals. When they talk big and boast, he just thinks they do it because they aren't sure of themselves and hope not so much to persuade others as to convince themselves.

The business exploits certain patent processes, notably the Sovereignty of Parliament and the Rule of Law.

The Sovereignty of Parliament means baldly that what Parliament says *goes*. There is no fundamental law with which it may not tamper, no rigid constitution that can be altered only by special machinery, and no Supreme Court can declare any Acts of Parliament illegal. Parliament can make, amend or repeal any law, great or small—the law of the constitution as easily as any other. And Parliament is

controlled by the people. Since 1928 the House of
Commons has been elected by adult suffrage; since
1911 the House of Lords has only a temporary veto
on measures passed by the Commons; and for more
than two centuries the Crown has had no veto at all.
So Parliament provides the machinery by which the
people can make or unmake law as they like and
therefore shape their freedom in whatever way they
may see fit.

The Rule of Law means that there is one law for
all men, that all men are equal before it, and that
no man can be punished except for the breach of it.
So the Rule of Law protects the freedom that the
people through Parliament have made.

Such in principle are John Bull's patent processes.
Now let's turn to the Management and Works and
see whether these principles are properly carried out.

The Crown at one period ran the whole firm. Even
later it took an active part in the management. But
with the rise of political parties, every political action
undertaken independently by the Crown became a
partisan act. If it pleased one party, it was bound to
displease another. So the Crown took shelter behind
ministerial responsibility and rose to a position above
parties. Such a position became all the more essential
when the Dominions achieved equality of status with
the Mother Country, for the Crown remained almost

the only legal authority common to the whole Empire. So the Crown is now the symbol of imperial unity and the constitutional Head of our own State. Heredity has been reconciled with democracy. For us it seems the only solution. The only alternative to an hereditary Crown is an elected President. But an elected President could obviously not be above party; his impartiality would therefore always be open to suspicion; and, since he would have been elected by one member of the Commonwealth only, he could not possibly be acceptable to other members as Head of the whole Empire.

The effective management of the business rests with the King's ministers, and the first thing that strikes one about them is the enormous powers they have managed to develop, thanks to the flexibility of our constitution, even outside their own proper executive sphere.

They sit in Parliament and control parliamentary legislation. They legislate *outside* Parliament, making Regulations which they proceed to apply themselves, thereby assuming judicial functions as well. To some extent all this is inevitable, even beneficial.

Owing to the complexity of our modern social laws, the government must be allowed to make *some* Regulations. But there's no excuse for the present orgy, and the Sovereignty of Parliament will be threatened unless the Commons exercise better control than at present. It is also inevitable that the government should to some extent *apply* its own Regulations, if only because the machinery of the ordinary law-courts is so costly and elaborate. But if our boasted Rule of Law is to be preserved, there ought at least to be a final appeal from the minister's decision to an independent court sitting in public.

Even in its own executive sphere the administration is constantly expanding. It can't be helped. All these new social laws involve more officials to work them. And as these laws increase our social freedom, I suppose we can't complain. But there's a danger in this growth of bureaucracy. I needn't labour the point. We've all had experience of pettifogging officialdom. The danger is that bureaucracy may eventually choke the very freedom it has been created to nurse. It tends to destroy individual initiative, to undermine responsibility and to lead to what has been called the Servile State, in which life becomes an officially conducted journey in a government charabanc from a state-rocked cradle to a state-dug grave. One would feel happier if, when indignation is aroused by some action of the police or other officials, the authorities were readier to take action. But no. Authorities are disposed to regard the very granting of an inquiry as a confession of their own guilt. Whereas actually, of course, it is a sign of vigilance and of their care for our freedom, and as such reassures the public.

So much for the Management. Now for the Works: Parliament and the Judiciary.

The Parliamentary machine is, of course, a triple affair, consisting of Crown, Lords and Commons. Of the Crown I have already spoken. It is a formal, rather than an active part of the machinery of Parliament. The House of Lords is an illogical survival. But in England that is hardly a serious objection. There are so many. And we thrive on them. It, too, is based on the hereditary principle. And, although its capacity for interference with democratic legislation has been rendered comparatively harmless, it certainly is nowadays something of an oddity. It survives, we are told, because few can be got to agree on any one particular scheme of reform, and such a fundamental change in the constitution ought only to come about by general agreement. But I suspect the true reason to be that we don't really need a second law-making body at all. A new one would have to be democratically elected. And we've already got one of those. A second might be a nuisance. What we really need is a sort of parliamentary annexe, a Council to tidy up the work done by the Commons and to do the type of work which the Commons hasn't either the time or the inclination to do itself. And for that you want a rather independent body of eminent people, which is not easily obtainable by any democratic method. So meanwhile the House of Lords carries on, doing very much the sort of work the ideal second chamber would do, and, in spite of every theoretical drawback, not doing it at all badly.

The House of Commons is, of course, the key-machine for making our liberty. As such it is overworked. Its output is limited to the political programme of the government, and even so it leaves an increasing amount of law-making to be done by the government itself. Many important matters that need long and careful debate have to be left to the House of Lords, and some—judicial reform, for instance—tend to get neglected altogether.

The machine works by the interplay of political parties, each of which is based on its own party machine. In the past neither of the two historical parties had a blameless record with regard to freedom. Conservatism stood for privilege; Liberalism for *laissez-faire*. Even nowadays parties are not perfect. Some say that the Conservative party is too much influenced by landed and moneyed interests; others that the Liberal party is a house divided against itself and no longer a party at all; others again that the Labour party rests on too narrow a basis and puts Trade Union before national interests. And all parties may be said at election time to dangle bribes rather unscrupulously under the noses of the electorate. Pensions, maybe, or protective tariffs— anything, as long as it's something for nothing. In the old days politicians bought their constituencies, but at least they paid for them themselves. Nowadays they still buy them, but the nation pays.

Still, the truth is surely that all three parties are sincerely and equally devoted to freedom, but to each of them freedom has a different meaning. That those several meanings have a lot in common, however, was shown in the debates over the Public Order Bill. Statesmen and newspapers expressed surprise and gratification at the unanimity with which all sections of the House approved of the principles of a Bill, which, it was carefully pointed out, was directed impartially at all extremists alike, whether Fascist or Communist. Let the dictators of Europe take note, it was suggested, how a democracy could not only protect its freedom, but discipline itself as well to prevent liberty lapsing into licence. True enough. But a *little* too smug, don't you think? I can imagine the dictators of Europe cynically observing that there was nothing so very surprising in the spectacle of a House representing three parties unanimously condemning two other parties which it barely represented at all.

Anyway, such liberty as we have is protected by the Judiciary. And the judicial machine in its principal parts is considered to be one of the best, if not *the* best, in the world. In fact, its fault lies in its very perfection. We could do with something more workmanlike and simple. The mass of law, the number of precedents, the elaborate procedure, make for delay, uncertainty and expense. It is rather as though, in order to crush a beetle, we had to take it to a steam-roller. It *does* crush the beetle beautifully, but the process takes a lot of time and costs a lot of money—especially if the beetle is in the provinces, because then it has to be sent all the way to London. For these troubles the cure seems to be a further codification of law, a simplification of procedure and a greater decentralisation of justice.

But when we turn to the lowest courts, the Petty Sessional Courts, which in their sphere are just as important as the higher courts, it can hardly be maintained that what they suffer from is too great perfection. In their case more radical reform is certainly necessary and overdue. And I think we are justified in being a little impatient about judicial reform. We boast about the Rule of Law. And that includes Equality before the Law. But in practice the law is beyond most people's means, and its expensiveness discriminates between rich and poor. We therefore pride ourselves on something which in fact we haven't got. And that's naughty.

Well, we've reviewed the Management and the Works. Now what about the product? Our Freedom, we saw, consists of Religious Liberty, Political Liberty and the Civil Liberties—Personal Freedom, Freedom of Expression and Freedom of Assembly and Association. They aren't perfect. They aren't quite complete. Bits of them are still missing; other bits are not very well defined. They are liable to be encroached upon at times by the Executive, and the Judiciary protects them only imperfectly. Still, taken as a whole, they are pretty good as far as they go. It's not the quality of our freedom we should complain of, so much as the quantity—its limitations. There are whole chunks left out. Social liberty, for instance. For large numbers of people it hardly exists at all. Certain occupations, certain educational opportunities, are open only to a minority. And in the economic sphere the majority of the nation has no say at all in the conduct of the concerns on which its livelihood depends. Many are without a livelihood at all. I feel you may well round on me and say: "Look here. You've been talking for hours about this wonderful Executive, Legislature and Judiciary, this beautiful Sovereignty of Parliament and Rule of Law, but all that this vast machinery can produce at the end of a thousand years or so is this small fragment of freedom. Why not scrap the whole works and set up something new?"

Now if our constitution was really just a machine, there'd be a great deal to be said for swapping it for a new one. For, regarded as a machine, it's a positive nightmare. It is old; parts of it are completely incongruous in modern times, and the original structure is barely recognisable, so many pieces have at various times been added or altered or removed. Just look what a muddle it's in. It consists of three parts, we say: Executive, Legislature and Judiciary. But, as we've just seen, the Executive legislates both inside and outside the Legislature and does a certain amount of judicial work as well. The Legislature contains the most important part of the Executive, the Ministry, and the most important of the Judiciary, for the Lord Chancellor presides over the House of Lords and the Law Lords are members of it. And as for the Judiciary, it legislates in the law courts, where it makes Common Law, and the heads of the three branches of the legal profession—the Chancellor, the Attorney-General and the Solicitor-General—are members of both the Executive and the Legislature. Every part of the constitution overlaps the other parts. They are all interlocked. And the whole thing is held together by a bewildering system of checks and balances. Would anybody in their senses make a machine like that? It couldn't work.

But the constitution *does* work—though not like a machine. A machine behaves mechanically. It obeys the laws of its construction and nothing else. It is not, for instance, sensitive to the behaviour of the people who work it, provided they observe those laws. But the constitution is *so* sensitive, that if any of those who work it fail to observe an indefinite number of customs, which can be broken without breaking the law, the whole system receives a shock and is thrown out of gear.[1] Again, a machine doesn't change—not of itself—not unless you do something to it. But the constitution is changing all the time, whether you do something to it or not. Compare, for instance, the status of the Dominions before and after the War. Before the War they were in several ways subordinate to the Mother Country. After the War they were her equals. Yet not a letter of the law had been changed. Since then, it is true, the Statute of Westminster has defined that change. But it only put on paper what was already established fact.

So this laborious metaphor of mine breaks down. The constitution *can't* be compared to a machine. It changes and grows and is sensitive like a living thing. And all its parts, with their checks and

[1] Instance the crisis of December 1936.

balances and interlocked functions, are like the organs of a body. We can only compare it properly with a living body. It is—and this is what I'm driving at— it is *organic*.

Now compare our constitution, organic and flexible, with a rigid constitution like that of the United States. A rigid constitution *is* like a machine. It doesn't grow. It doesn't change—unless you do something to it. A rigid constitution defines freedom in the constitutional document and says, in effect: "This is the freedom which citizens shall enjoy for all time." So that, to take the case of the United States, a twentieth-century people may be bound by the ideals of its eighteenth-century ancestors. The constitution can only be altered by special machinery, which adds a bit to, or takes a bit from, the old machine. But our constitution has no such rigid form and contains no such rigid definitions. It is just a living body with organs capable of producing freedom. And it is at all times up to the citizens to produce it.

That's one good reason for carrying on with it rather than swapping it even for the best mechanical constitution which is rigid. And we can't swap it for another as flexible as ours, because they can't be made. They have to grow. And you know how long it has taken ours to grow even into what it is now. And, if we complain, as we're entitled to, that what it is now isn't good enough, this organic conception of it will not only explain why it is no better than it is, but reassure us as to the future. Let's see.

The organ that produces our freedom is Parliament. Parliament has been growing for centuries and producing freedom for centuries. But it naturally only produces the freedom required by those who control it. The comparatively few who controlled it in the past didn't require social liberty. They had it already. But they did require civil liberties, because in their struggle against arbitrary government security before the law was essential. So our civil liberties came first. Religious liberty they also needed. But Roman Catholics and Protestant Dissenters were alike excluded from Parliament. So, though they were powerful enough in other ways to secure practical toleration fairly soon, they didn't secure religious equality till the last century. By then it was clear that liberty could only be won by those who controlled the liberty-making organ. So then began the struggle for political liberty. It was got by degrees. The final victory came with adult suffrage in 1928. And it is only since then—less than ten years ago—that the whole nation has controlled Parliament and is therefore in a position to make Parliament produce the social and other freedom that the nation as a whole requires.

As a result of all these changes, the word "liberty" itself has changed its meaning. Originally, you may remember, liberty didn't mean freedom. A liberty meant a privilege. Liberties were exceptional privileges which certain kinds of people had a fundamental right to. In fact, we may say that the creation of liberty consisted in the abolition of liberties. In the fifteenth century we had to fight the liberties of the Barons, in the sixteenth the liberties of the Church, in the seventeenth the liberties or Prerogatives of the Crown, and in the eighteenth the liberties or privileges of an unrepresentative Parliament. With the movement for parliamentary reform the word began to have a new meaning. When John Wilkes talked about liberty, he meant religious, political and civil freedom—more or less what we've got to-day. Notice that to Englishmen the word, in spite of the change in its meaning, still stood for something positive and concrete. But the French, under Rousseau's influence chiefly, adopted an abstract, philosophical meaning. "La Liberté" to them meant the Rights of Man. And they had disciples in England, notably Tom Paine. But though this foreign notion caught on for a time, it didn't last. It was too vague, too nebulous, for Englishmen.

They preferred to follow their own bent, and the two thinkers who influenced them most were Edmund

Burke before the French Revolution and Jeremy Bentham after it. The Rights of Man were just bunk to both of them. Bentham set nineteenth-century England on the more prosaic path of Individualism, *Laissez-faire* and no nonsense. Freedom meant to do as you please. Liberty in short was Liberty Hall. Free contract, the abolition of privileges and manhood suffrage. The Liberal party throughout the century put the programme into effect. And, with reservations, the net result was what Dicey summed up so brilliantly in his famous book: *The Law of the Constitution*.

Liberty according to Dicey. It's a landmark. It marks the end of a period. One or two things still remained undone to complete his picture—adult suffrage, for instance. And one or two things had already happened that found no place in his design —the kind of social legislation which he called "collectivism". But he made a pattern, a classical pattern of liberty as it was at the end of the nineteenth century. "Democracy tempered with snobbishness" (to use his own description). The Sovereignty of Parliament, the Rule of Law, Religious, Civil and Political Liberty—that was the whole of Freedom. So I was taught in my youth and so I implicitly believed. And I think it is still the prevailing belief even now.

You may say: 'That's all nonsense. Few people have ever heard of Dicey. And, anyway, he's dead!' Yes. But the thoughts that great men think live after them and filter down gradually into the sub-consciousness of ordinary people to a quite uncanny extent. Bentham's influence outlived him for fifty years at least. Dicey's influence is still with us. You remember that street-hawker I spoke of in my first talk. How did *he* define freedom? "Not being messed about by Government or coppers." Well, that was pure Bentham. It was also freedom *à la* Dicey, more or less.

But Dicey's pattern no longer serves our purpose. It is too narrow. It doesn't include social or economic liberty at all—perhaps because in his day there was so little of it that it escaped his notice. If we drew a graph to-day to represent the amount of liberty we possess of various kinds, civil, religious and political liberties would stick up like mountain peaks, but the line would sag badly when it came to judicial liberty, and only deep valleys of depression would mark economic and social freedom.

Freedom like that is a poor thing, incomplete and miserly—a personal, not a social possession. Each of us has his own private box of freedom. Owing to distinctions of class and wealth, some are big boxes and some are small. I mustn't interfere with yours, nor you with mine. But otherwise we've got very little responsibility towards each other's boxes, except that we all have to contribute something to a common poor box. Each man's box is his own private privilege. The old conception of liberty as a privilege still sticks to it even now. Our liberties are our fundamental rights. And Society is a clash of rights. Individual *versus* Individual, Capital *versus* Labour, the Free Man *versus* the State. Democracy means "I'm as good as you", not "You're as good as me". And every one of us stands on his own Tom Tiddler's ground ready to pounce on the trespasser.

The trouble about this attitude is that it regards freedom as a right, but disregards the obligations that attach to it. The lone wolf is free, but he has no rights. Our freedom is our right, because the state protects it, and in return for that protection we owe certain obligations to the state. There can be no rights without obligations.

Even in the old days, when liberty didn't pretend to mean more than privilege, people got their privileges in return for certain services. The baron had his liberties in return for certain services to his overlord, and so on throughout society. Liberty was the reward of service. That was its origin in England. It's a pity that's been lost sight of. We don't do much service for our liberty nowadays, and we resent the little we have to do. The obligations we owe to the state in return for the rights it guarantees to us are mainly negative. Most of our laws tell us what we *mustn't* do—murder, steal, slander, and so on. The things we *must* do are few, and, with the exception of paying rates and taxes, paltry. We must assist a constable if called upon to do so, help to quell a riot whether we're called upon or not, sit on a jury, give evidence in court, reveal treason, if we hear of any, and fill in a few forms occasionally. That's about all our compulsory, positive obligations.

It looks, therefore, as if the negative view of freedom as a right without positive obligations had pretty well triumphed. But, although our *compulsory* obligations are few, we *voluntarily* incur any amount of other responsibilities. In fact, unless we sit very still and do nothing, it's almost impossible to avoid them. If we join the army, become a doctor, run a business, make a contract, build a house, employ labour, have children, or do almost anything, we incur any number of obligations. And although it's true that we incur them voluntarily, the state has in recent times so closely circumscribed our every action, that the negative view of freedom as a right without obligations no longer fits the facts.

And, again, the problem of liberty can no longer be stated in such simple terms as a struggle between the free man and the state. There are other factors now to be taken into account. Between the individual and the state there have grown up and interposed themselves all sorts of groups—Trade Unions, big industries, semi-socialised corporations, and so on. These, too, have their rights and obligations in relation to the state just as the individual has. In fact, the state deals almost as much with groups as with individuals. The individual tends to get lost in the group, or groups, to which he belongs, and the state to become rather a collection of groups than of individuals. So if we persist in regarding liberty as a right without obligations and the individual as a sort of lone wolf, we're forced to conclude that he's getting the worst of it. In which case there's less freedom than there was. But is there? Our old liberties, civil and religious, are at least as good as they were; our political liberty is better; and, though there's not much to be said for our social liberty, it's anyway not as bad as it was.

So, to sum up, "The Free Man *versus* the State" is nowadays a nonsensical formula, and Dicey's pattern of freedom is incomplete. Sovereignty of Parliament and Rule of Law are grand things. The one enables us to make our freedom, the other protects it when made. Civil, religious and political freedoms have been made and are, more or less, protected. And they're grand things too. But there are other freedoms which are only partially made and hardly protected at all. And Dicey doesn't tell us how to complete them. He leads us up a lovely garden path. But there's no stately mansion at the end, not even a nice little cottage with roses round the door—only a half-built villa. In fact, Dicey's garden path reminds me of an avenue I saw not long ago on the outskirts of London. It was a pretty avenue, with grass and young trees and flowering shrubs down each side. But it only led to waste ground littered with pots and pans and rubbish. It was a building estate. The future roads were still only tracks of ploughed up earth. And in each road was only one half-built villa with an enormous hoarding beside it. I read one of these advertisements. It said: "Baronial Halls for the People. £5 deposit and 12s. 6d. a week. Choose your home in Nature's Bond Street."

Freedom *à la* Dicey is rather like that. It's incomplete, and it's given us a wrong conception of freedom. But liberty hadn't always meant even what it meant to Dicey. It had changed its meaning before then. It can change it again. And I think it *is* changing it now. Look at it in this way.

Freedom conceived as a struggle between the Free Man and the State means just this. That a man, free from interference, can do just as much as he is capable of doing all by himself. But isn't it conceivable that Society could be so organised as to give him greater opportunities for doing things? You may be free to swim in a river full of alligators, but you won't have much fun. Wouldn't you have more freedom and more fun, if the state removed the alligators?

The Free Man *versus* the State seems to me, therefore, a silly proposition. Any amount of state interference is permissible, provided it creates more freedom for the individual. That's the answer to the old question: Does the state exist for the individual, or the individual for the state? The state, of course, exists for *all* the individuals in the state. Therefore, it must not discriminate between them. And in so far as it does discriminate, it fails in its function. So freedom, we might say, is at its best when the state has created conditions in which all citizens without discrimination have the greatest possible opportunities for self-expression.

At the moment there's a great deal of discrimination, isn't there? And a great deal of state interference would be necessary to remove it. More state interference means more restraint of individuals. But restraint is only justifiable if it creates more freedom. How then can greater interference by the state be reconciled with greater liberty of the individual? There's the rub.

XI

THE FREE MAN IN SOCIETY

FREEDOM, then, is not a discord of individual clashes
of Free Men *versus* the State, but a collective harmony
of Free Men in Society. Such a harmony would mean
more freedom, but it would also mean more state
interference to secure it. How then can we reconcile
greater freedom with greater restraint?

Perhaps we can't. The Communist says we can't,
if we stick to our liberal democracy. The Fascist says
we can't anyhow. If either of them is right, it's no
good going on as we are. We're only wasting time.
Let's see.

Few books have so profoundly influenced civilisation
as Karl Marx's *Das Kapital*; the Russian Revolution
is the most important political event since the French
Revolution; and Bolshevism is the greatest social
experiment in history. Yet Marx's philosophy was
somebody else's turned upside down; his history was
lopsided; his economics were cock-eyed; and his
doctrine, which started as a hard-headed protest
against the visionary idealism and vague sentimen-

talities of earlier Socialists, ended in a final state of society just as visionary, idealistic, vague and sentimental.

According to him, all history had been a succession of struggles between various classes for control of the means of production. Whatever class temporarily controlled the means of production automatically controlled everything else and exploited everything and everybody in its own interests. The last stage of that struggle had now been reached. The bourgeois capitalist was opposed by the proletarian worker. Capital would become concentrated in fewer and fewer hands, and the condition of the worker would become steadily worse. Revolution was inevitable, and the victory of the workers assured. A proletarian dictatorship would follow. The means of production would be socialised and all other classes suppressed. When they had finally disappeared, the state, which was only an instrument by which one class could bully another, would have become superfluous. It would "wither away". "The necessity of observing the simple fundamental rules of social life would have become a habit."[1] "Each would work voluntarily according to his ability, and each would take freely according to his needs."[2] And mankind would live happily ever after.

[1] Engels.   [2] Lenin.

Now, except for the fairy-tale ending, which may well be doubted but cannot be disproved, every step in that argument is at least partially false. But, if it it isn't true, it contains a lot of truth. And it is so much simpler than the truth. Half-truths usually are. If labour were the only source of value, as he said, then the worker produced more than he was paid for. Labour, we know, isn't the only source of value, but that doesn't alter the fact that labour in Marx's time wasn't getting fair do's. Again, history is not merely the story of class struggles, but throughout history there have been class inequalities. And in narrowing down the issue to economic organisation, Marx was only emphasising the most glaring inequalities of all. Add to this the underlying optimism of his doctrine—namely that the worker was bound to win anyway and inherit a promised land of a free and equal society with plenty and to spare for all—and you can see why this half-truth had such a wide appeal.

Yet for a long time it didn't make much headway. Social conditions in most countries improved instead of getting worse as Marx had prophesied. Besides, revolution isn't easy nowadays, and, if it comes, it doesn't necessarily lead to Communism. Russia, with her undeveloped industries and her population of recently liberated serfs, was entirely exceptional.

Tsarist rule was outrageous; it was also incompetent. There was the misery caused by the War and the discontent of an abominably ill-used army. All that was abnormal. So revolution was successful, hundreds of thousands were killed; and literally millions starved. Twenty years have passed; there is still a scarcity of some of the necessaries of life; and much that is plentiful is shoddy. But the means of production have been more or less socialised, and Bolshevism has reached Marx's second stage on the road to Communism, namely the Dictatorship of the Proletariat.

At least, that's what we're told. Actually, behind the window-dressing of the present constitution as of the new one promised, which is more democratic in form, all effective power is concentrated in a governing minority, the Communist party, which consists of less than three per cent. of the population. Its members enjoy priority and privileges in respect of food, housing, amusements, transport, and so on. They occupy all important positions in the bureaucracy which is the real machinery of government. They dominate the Army, the Police and the Press. And their chiefs form the complicated Executive, in which all authority is centralised, subject to the autocracy of the Dictator himself.

Until the people are educated up to the Communist

creed, we are told, the enlightened minority must act for them. It does for the people what the people would do for themselves, if only they thought rightly. It only dragoons and persecutes in the name of truth. But so did the Spanish Inquisition. And, if this is only a temporary necessity during a transitional stage, how long will it last? We can't say, is the answer, but a very long time. The leaders themselves say so. And we may well believe them. When has a dictator, or an aristocracy, ever felt that the moment had come to surrender authority? And in this case the moment seems particularly remote. For no Communist has ever attempted to define the ultimate organisation of Communist society. The state, it is said, will "wither away". And "the authority of government over persons will be replaced by the administration of things".[1] But how? When? Why? Nobody knows. It looks as though Russians must wait, like the Jews, for the millennium. Will they, do you think?

The more one reads about Bolshevism, the more one is astonished—partly horrified, partly filled with admiration, but wholly bewildered. It is barbarous, and it is ultra-modern. It is completely materialistic, yet it is saturated with idealism. It is atheistic, but it has all the fanaticism of a religion. It is tyrannical, but in the name of freedom. It is largely oriental, yet

[1] Engels.

217

it calls all the bluff of western civilisation. And *that*, I think, is its essence. I don't believe in it. In many ways it revolts me. But I do feel that it makes a lot of the current coinage of our social creed sound like dud half-crowns on a counter.

And what about Fascism? That's downright enough anyway. No nonsense about philosophy or logic. "Intuition", writes one enthusiast, "is the very basis, as well as the highest form of knowledge."[1] And another: "Fascism as an idea is undefinable. It is a fact which is taking place."[2] The "fact" came as a reaction against the inefficiency and corruption of democratic politics in Italy. Authority, it was claimed, was necessary—authority and an alternative system of government. It found them both in history. From the Roman Empire it took Caesarism—dictatorship and centralised authority; from the Roman Church a hierarchy of officials and a vague mysticism, and from the City States of mediaeval Italy a corporative organisation of society. "To believe, to obey, to fight"—"Order, discipline, authority"—those are its two chief slogans. And its object, we are told, is to "subordinate the activity and interests of the individual citizen to the general interests of the nation".

[1] J. S. Barnes, *Fascism*, p. 65.
[2] Marriott, *Dictatorship and Democracy*, p. 193.

218

The interesting thing about it from our point of view is its corporative organisation, which is something like syndicalism and guild socialism. And if it were what it pretends to be, it would be a very valuable social experiment. Unfortunately it isn't. The syndicates are so constituted that the interests of employers are paramount over those of the workers, and all effective power, as in Russia, is in the hands of a minority party entrenched in a bureaucracy and surmounted by a dictator.

The consequences to date are not encouraging. Unemployment has been terrible, wages are low, and the standard of living worse. The effect on foreign trade has driven the government to seek self-sufficiency as the only solution. Economic self-sufficiency has been reinforced by the regimentation of all citizens from childhood. The result is a very self-conscious nationalism and an excellent organisation for war, but a poor organisation for national welfare in times of peace. There is, of course, no freedom. "We have buried the putrid corpse of liberty", says Signor Mussolini.

Germany has buried it, too. National Socialism triumphed there as a protest against depression, defeatism and the humiliation at Versailles. It has certainly restored national prestige and self-respect. It has as yet not gone so far as Italy towards syndicalism. Towards militarism and self-sufficiency it has gone even further. And it has added one new feature —Racialism. And that's odd, when you come to think of it. Fascism had a genuine historical background in the Caesarism of Rome. But Germany's ancestor-worship is largely fake. The Nordic myth comes strangely from a nation at least half of which is of alpine stock. And anyway those alleged Nordic ancestors prided themselves on their freedom. The last thing they would have put up with would have been dictatorship or regimentation.

Still, there it is. Germany has followed Italy. Austria and other countries have half-heartedly followed both. Bits of China have half-heartedly followed Russia. And the world drifts nearer to a holy war between Communism and Fascism. And yet, you know, stripped of their theories, they have in practice much in common. In Russia, Italy and Germany alike the net result is a national revival, an intense earnestness of purpose, and a loss of sense of humour. Each is ruled by a dictator, an exclusive and privileged minority, and a bureaucracy. Authority is based on force, fear and propaganda. All three are militaristic and intolerant. There is no liberty, whether civil or political. All citizens are conscripted and dragooned in body and mind from early childhood, and their present welfare is sacrificed to a future ideal, vague and perhaps unrealisable. You may say, "That's not fair. Communism and Fascism are in an experimental or transitional stage." But then so are we. And we can only judge them—as we expect to be judged—by what they have been and are, not by what they profess to be or hope to become.

Still, there remains one argument we haven't yet faced. Fascism and Communism both claim that they at least have something to hope for, but liberal democracy hasn't. Fascists argue that democracies will never get anywhere. They are, to begin with, decadent. Are they? Great Britain, Canada, Australia, New Zealand, South Africa, France, Belgium, Switzerland, Holland, Denmark, Norway, Sweden, the United States. Not a bad bunch surely. Hardly decadent. Further, say the Fascists, democracy is slow, inefficient and undisciplined. Is *that* true? What about our own last serious crises—1931 and December 1936? Not one of these adjectives applies, does it? In fact, at the risk of being rude, we might turn the tables on Italy and Germany and say: "When you say that democracy is all these things, what you really mean is that your *own* democracies were. Democracy, as we know, is the hardest form of government to work. You have to be good at it. You weren't. And people who aren't up to the best form of government naturally have to put up with something inferior." Of course, when it comes to a change of policy, democracy is *slower* than a dictatorship, because with the latter only one man has to change his mind, whereas in the former millions have to. So democratic policy is more consistent, Fascist more opportunist. In the smash and grab times we live in, opportunism has many advantages. But consistency is usually reckoned the finer virtue, and it has yet to be proved that it doesn't pay best in the end.

The Communist line of attack is that social justice will never be won in our liberal democracy, because those who control the means of production always control everything else. So the bourgeois capitalist will go on exploiting the proletarian worker till the crack of revolution. In short, economic power controls political power. Well, there's some truth in that. But there's more in the opposite. Political power controls economic power. That was proved when the middle classes got the vote in the nineteenth century. It was proved again after the further extensions of the franchise in 1884 and 1918. For between 1890 and 1927 expenditure on social services, even allowing for the fall in the value of the currency, increased at least sevenfold. Since 1928 we've *all* got votes. And that explains why we didn't all get social justice before and why we *can* all get it now.

If that is so, let's get on with it. But how? On what

lines? Well, there's no need to be dogmatic. I distrust all dogmatically framed systems of society—Communism, Socialism, Fascism—all the "isms". You can't stuff humanity into a mould. That's why these advertisers of patent social systems don't really deal with humanity at all. They use dummies instead. Dummies are easier to handle, and you can make them fit your mould. A "Capitalist" for instance—as a living person he's hard to define, and he will change so. Think of him in the early days of the Industrial Revolution, in Marx's day, in our own day. Not the the same chap at all. No good for a mould. Let's use dummies instead, say the system-makers. Let them all be dummies—Capitalist, Bourgeois, Proletariat and the rest of them. Aunt Sallies all, and a penny a shy.

But, if we don't need a system to work to, we must have a principle to work by. What's it to be? Well, we found one at the end of my last talk. It was this. Freedom is at its best when all citizens without discrimination have the greatest possible opportunities for self-expression. In short, Equality of Opportunity —there's our principle.

Equality of Opportunity—not Equality, mind you. Men are not equally endowed by nature, and we can't make them so. But we can remove inequalities that are not natural but artificial, so that as far as possible all men may have equal chances to use what natural endowments they possess. I say "as far as possible", because there are limits. Take environment, for instance. Some places are healthier than others. Or take the family. Some parents are better than others. You may want to make further qualifications. It is arguable, for instance, that a man should be allowed to amass savings and bequeath them at his death, because this is an incentive to industry and therefore has social value. All such qualifications mean, of course, that some will get a better start in life than others. But, subject to such qualifications, the principle is that in life's race all should start scratch.

Yes. But the strong will forge ahead, and the weak get left hoplessly behind, perhaps below subsistence level. They may even be exploited by the strong. So our principle needs further qualification. The freedom of some must be restrained to preserve the freedom of all. There must be a respectable minimum level of livelihood below which no citizen is allowed to fall. That done, the individual can be given his head. Exceptional ability deserves exceptional recognition, as an incentive for its exercise and as a reward for its achievements. But here again there are limits. We are entitled to discourage activities which are socially harmful and to scale the reward for other activities in proportion to their social value. So it comes to this. A reasonable minimum provision for all and a maximum reward for work measured by its social value—these are respectively the lower and upper limitations proper to individual enterprise. But between this floor and this ceiling individual enterprise should be encouraged to the utmost.

Of course, opinions will differ as to the proper levels of floor and ceiling. The champions of individual liberty will want to give the individual as much head room as possible. Those whose preferences are for man in the mass will want a high floor and a low ceiling. And finally there are the busybodies, faddists and spoil-sports who would bury freedom in a shallow coffin. But most of us, though we don't ask for the freedom of the bandit, *do* want to be Free Men in Society.

The Free Man in Society. That's it. Some will put the accent on the Free Man, others will put it on Society. But the *principle* of equality of opportunity is so patently just that it is difficult to avoid accepting it, even if we boggle rather at some of the consequences that follow from its acceptance. It is, indeed, accepted tacitly, if not openly, by all three of our principal political parties. If you read *The Socialist Movement* by Mr Ramsay Macdonald and *Liberalism* by Professor Hobhouse, both of which books were published in

1911, you will find that their conclusions are practically identical. Equality of opportunity is implicit in both. And since the War the general principles of legislation advocated by all three parties have tended to converge still more closely. Each may still cling to fragments of what have been historically its pet theories, but nothing has been more striking during the past year than the very general agreement on the right course to pursue. Parties differ mainly as to the details of the route and the pace to be set.

The pace to be set. That's the difficulty. You see, we believe that change must come by consent, not by force. You can't *force* men to be free, we say. You can only persuade them. Persuasion or force. That's the real cleavage between us on the one side and Fascism and Communism on the other. I think we're right. But we've got to prove it. And since 1928 freedom is within our grasp. It's our fault now if we don't get it. And we must get it as quickly as we can, as a matter of social justice and to justify our democracy.

For EU product safety concerns, contact us at Calle de José Abascal, 56–1°, 28003 Madrid, Spain or eugpsr@cambridge.org.

www.ingramcontent.com/pod-product-compliance
Ingram Content Group UK Ltd.
Pitfield, Milton Keynes, MK11 3LW, UK
UKHW012331130625
459647UK00009B/199